Winning With Your Voice

Morton Cooper, Ph.D

FELL PUBLISHERS, INC.
Hollywood, Florida

NOTE: Although some of the names have been changed, all of the case histories are factual.

Copyright © 1990 Morton Cooper, Ph.D.

For information address:
Fell Publishers, Inc.
2131 Hollywood Blvd.
Hollywood, Florida 33020

Published simultaneously in Canada by
Prentice-Hall Canada, Toronto

Library of Congress Cataloging-in-Publication Data

Cooper, Morton. 1931–
    Winning with your voice / by Morton Cooper. — Rev. ed.
        p.   cm.
    ISBN 0-8119-0660-4 : $17.95. — ISBN 0-8119-0723-6 (pbk.) : $12.95
    1. Voice culture.   I. Title
PN4162.C66   1990
808.5—dc20

                                                          90-3089
                                                            CIP

Acknowledgement

There are numerous people to whom I am indebted, especially the many patients who have encouraged me to write about my new voice techniques so that others can also benefit and who have allowed their stories to be told. In addition, I am grateful to the celebrity patients who have allowed their names to be mentioned over the years. Their public acknowledgement of voice help has alerted an unknowing public to this field and has encouraged individuals with voice problems to seek assistance. I also want to express the extreme gratitude to patients with spastic dysphonia and paralytic dysphonia who have told their stories using their real first names in Chapter Nine.

I must make note here of the individuals from different disciplines, especially physicians, psychologists, speech pathologists, teachers of singing, and former patients, who have referred patients to me over the years. Specific colleagues whose assistance, friendship, or guidance have given me the support and faith I needed in order to develop in my field are: Virgil Anderson, Ph.D., Robert West, Ph.D., Lee Travis, Ph.D., Joel Pressman, M.D., Henry J. Rubin, M.D., John Snidecor, Ph.D., Elise Hahn, Ph.D., Nobuhiko Isshiki, M.D., Benjamin Kagen, M.D., and Gershon Lesser, M.D.

To the American Speech-Language-Hearing Association, for providing an ear and a forum, over the years, to my revolutionary natural approach to voice training, covering a range of hitherto ignored voice disorders. And to the many thousands of speech and language pathologists and audiologists who provide better speech, hearing, and communication through their needed services to the public. I am indebted to them for their many kindnesses and willingness to hear my views. Here's hoping they will use my simple, innovative techniques to help people find better voices or improve troubled voices.

Acknowledgement

To Continental Cable and Century Cable, for affording Public Access programing to present the areas of voice and speech to the general public for the past six years.

Also, I want to thank specific people for their contribution in bringing this book to life:

Marcia Ann Hartung Cooper, M.A., my wife, also a speech pathologist, for helping me express and define my thoughts of voice training and voice rehabilitation in this book and in many other books and articles over the past twenty-five years.

The staff at Fell Publishers: Donald Lessne, publisher, for his trust and support in publishing this book; Barbara Newman, speech pathologist, who recommended this book so highly that she made the publication possible; Elizabeth Wyatt, editor of the first edition, and Allan Taber, editor of the revised edition, for bringing a sharper focus and a clearer perception of what *Winning With Your Voice* is about; and Johanna Porter-Connell, art director, who was able to translate my crude sketches into polished visuals; Joe Madden, art director, who designed the eye catching jacket for the revised edition, and Halyna Shafranski, who brought it all together.

Fred Basten, for his literary assistance in organizing reams of my material and his outstanding ability in putting form to it.

Wanda Sue Parrott, for her suggestions and organization of the early draft in the area of public speaking.

Jim Heacock, for his persistence in finding me the right publisher who really believes in *Winning With Your Voice*.

Irwin Zucker, for being a mainstay in getting me heard, listened to and read.

Cheryl B. Dupuy, M.S., for her helpful suggestions after reading portions of the manuscript.

Hettie Tack for her secretarial assistance.

Nancy Lamb, Photography, Santa Monica, CA, for the cover photo.

Marla and Lorna Cooper, for typing the manuscript on the computer.

I greatly value the assistance or encouragement of each of the above named individuals. I hope finding your Winning Voice gives you as much pleasure as I receive from watching my patients find their voices, and that you go on to a more successful and satisfying life, professionally and socially.

About the Author

Morton Cooper has been helping people find strong, healthy, natural, and attractive voices for more than thirty years, utilizing a program of Direct Voice Rehabilitation and Training which he developed. His techniques have enabled countless people to find their natural voices in seconds and, with practice, develop effective, winning voices. His unique program has helped thousands of people with voice problems regain their voices and resume their lives after many had been told their cases were virtually hopeless.

Dr. Cooper developed an interest in the speaking voice when he lost his own voice after two well-meaning college professors told him to use a deep throat voice to replace his own nasal-sounding voice. He developed persistent laryngitis, tired voice, throat clearing, and had difficulty being heard, all classic symptoms of the misused voice. After seeing twelve physicians who ran him through a gamut of tests and told him, among other things, he was dying of cancer, the thirteenth doctor actually listened to his voice and understood that the problem was being caused by a misused speaking voice. After a few months of voice training, the symptoms were abating and the voice was coming back, at which point Dr. Cooper decided to do his graduate studies specializing in speech and the speaking voice. Based on his own experiences, he decided to help others help themselves, and over a number of years developed his simple, revolutionary techniques to a "winning voice."

Dr. Cooper is a licensed Speech Pathologist in California and is certified by the American Speech-Language-Hearing Association (ASHA). He received a certification of appreciation from ASHA that reads, "in recognition of a significant contribution to the American Speech-Language-Hearing Association and to the profession of speech pathology and audiology." He has been the Director of the Voice and Speech Clinic at UCLA Medical Center and a Clinical Assistant Professor of the Head and Neck Division at UCLA Medical Center. He was Director of the Adult Stutterers Group at Stanford University.

He is a consultant and regular speaker at the Pritikin Longevity Center. He has written regular columns for publications, as well as chapters in several leading speech pathology handbooks. His textbook *Modern Techniques of Vocal Rehabilitation* has been used for the past seventeen years as a college text throughout the world.

Dr. Cooper has appeared on numerous television talk shows including: *The Oprah Winfrey Show, The Today Show, Good Morning America, CNN, The Merv Griffin Show, Hour Magazine*, Regis Philbin, and Joe Franklin. On radio, Dr. Cooper has been heard nationally with Larry King, Michael Jackson, Ray Briem, Owen Spann, and many others.

Interviews with Dr. Cooper regarding his techniques have been published in *USA Today, The Los Angeles Times, The Washington Post, US Magazine, Mademoiselle* magazine, *The New York Times Sunday Magazine*, and *The Wall Street Journal*. His studies and papers have been published in the *Journal of Speech and Hearing Disorders, Archives of Otolaryngology, California Medicine, Medical Tribune, Pediatric News, Eye, Ear, Nose and Throat Monthly, Journal of Communication Disorders, Journal of Fluency Disorders, Voices: The Art and Science of Psychotherapy, Geriatrics, Grade Teacher, Bulletin of the National Association of Teachers of Singing, Music Educators Journal, Education, Prevention, Case and Comment, Trial, Screen Actor, The Quill*, and others.

He has traveled extensively, speaking at many colleges and universities; he has been a speaker at numerous medical facilities including Cedars-Sinai Medical Center, UCLA Medical Center, St. John's Hospital, White Memorial Medical Center, Walter Reed Army Hospital and Kaiser-Permanente Hospital, and at many medical groups, including the Los Angeles Neurological Society, the Los Angeles Society of Otolaryngology, and the Ross-Loos Medical Group. Dr. Cooper received a bachelor's degree from Brooklyn College, a master's degree from Indiana University, a doctorate degree from the University of California at Los Angeles, and also studied at Stanford University.

He and his wife Marcia, also a speech pathologist, live in Los Angeles. They have two daughters, Lorna and Marla.

His previous book, *Change Your Voice, Change Your Life*, is now in its tenth printing.

Dr. Cooper is in private practice in West Los Angeles, California. He can be reached at 10921 Wilshire Blvd., Suite 401, Los Angeles, CA 90024 or phone (213) 208-6047.

Audio and video cassettes of Dr. Cooper's techniques are now available. For information, use the above address or phone number.

Contents

Introduction

In today's high-tech world of sound, no other means of communication surpasses the human voice. Yet Dr. Cooper estimates twenty-five percent of all Americans use a voice too low in their throats and fifty percent use a voice that is too high, nasal and thin, ruining the chances of success for many people. They ignore the warning signals of trouble ahead and go through life unheard and unappreciated.

Here in this invaluable guide, Dr. Morton Cooper reveals his step-by-step plan for success through correct voice techniques. Using his basic exercises, it takes only seconds essentially to find your natural, effective voice, then only minutes a day of practice to keep it. He discusses simple, direct ways to control the major parameters of voice, and thereby to have a "winning voice."

Over the years, Dr. Cooper's innovative approach to a "winning voice" has been used successfully by men and women of all ages, from all walks of life. These techniques have been used by such notables as Anne Bancroft, Henry Fonda, Joan Rivers, Lucille Ball, Richard Crenna, Cheryl Ladd, O.J. Simpson, entrepreneur and art collector Norton Simon, Rosey Grier, singer Stevie Nicks, and Diahann Carroll, among others.

Nearly everyone has a hidden "star quality" voice that is strong, full and effective. Most people don't use the voice potential they have because they don't realize it's there. From childhood on, they ignore their voices. They grow up with voices that misrepresent them, that detract from who they really are, and that may create voice problems.

One voice problem, spastic dysphonia, is the most controversial of all, because most consider the causation to be neurological, and treat by surgery and botulinum. Since Dr. Cooper has found this voice problem to be caused basically by voice misuse and abuse, with psychological overtones, he has greatly expanded the section in this book on spastic dysphonia and its treatment by Direct Voice Rehabilitation. He is currently working with UCLA Medical Center, Head and Neck Division, on voice studies, especially spastic dysphonia.

This revised edition also offers a new approach to help beginners learn how to talk in public. Almost everyone is concerned, anxious, or nervous about talking in public, or giving a speech. Dr. Cooper's approach helps take away the fears beginners experience when asked to speak in public. A greatly enlarged chapter has been added to *Winning With Your Voice* to explain simply and directly how you, as a beginner, can talk in public and like it, as simple as 1,2,3.

In addition, Dr. Cooper has worked with stutterers in groups and individually through the years, finding that stuttering is essentially caused by misconceptions and myths, not heredity or neurological factors. Dr. Cooper explains why stutterers stutter and what can be done to help them talk normally.

Winning With Your Voice will show you how to have a stronger, healthier voice that should have more authority, be more outgoing and more easily understood, and how to talk in public and like it. It is a book for everyone who has to talk (like it or not) and wants to make a positive impression on others. Discover how to find and develop your "Winning Voice."

Quotes

WINNING WITH YOUR VOICE

"Mort Cooper is a voice computer genius. Finding a new method to help people to discover the innate power of their own voices and speech has made him the foremost speech therapist in the world."

—Harold Robbins, Best Selling Author

"Dr. Cooper makes your real voice happen in seconds."

—Harvey Mackay, Author of *Swim with the Sharks Without Being Eaten Alive* and *Beware the Naked Man Who Offers You His Shirt*

L. to R.: HARVEY MACKAY, IRWIN ZUCKER (PUBLICIST), MORTON COOPER, Ph.D., and CAROL ANN MACKAY.

Chapter 1

The Power of a Winning Voice

WHEN YOU SAY "HELLO," DOES YOUR VOICE SAY "GOODBYE"?

What a powerful force we have in our voices. It is, by far, our most important feature for presenting ourselves to others. A rich, full voice turns frowns into smiles, opens closed doors, wins friends and influences people. It is heard, listened to and liked, and has the power to enhance the quality of a person's life. It can work miracles.

An unpleasant sounding voice can be devastating. It can lead to family arguments or friction in a romance. It can sour business deals and promotions. A troubled or wrong voice can create unintentional stumbling blocks by turning people off.

Every day, ads promote the latest in electronic communications equipment designed to make working easier and our lives more enjoyable. Yet for all the advanced wizardry, nothing can compete with the sound of the human voice. It is still, by far, the greatest communicator of all.

A misused voice tells a lot about you, probably more than you care to tell. Have you heard yourself when you are depressed? When you are elated? When you are afraid or nervous? A wrong voice relays many messages, even those that are best kept to yourself. This is discussed in detail in Chapter 4.

1

When Henry Kissinger talks, there is a sense of doom and gloom, even when his words are optimistic. Do you hear authority? Do you hear self-assurance? I believe he wants us to feel he is in control; but the sound may be too controlled and his voice may not be representing him as best it could.

I hear Erma Bombeck once said, "If you miss the first few words of Henry Kissinger, forget it, folks!" Kissinger's voice may very well make us tune out. It doesn't come alive because he uses it incorrectly, letting it sag in the lower throat. He speaks from "down deep," trudging along as though he is out of breath, and out of energy.

When James Bond talks, through Roger Moore, we listen. Roger Moore speaks low, much like Henry Kissinger, but Moore's voice energizes us. It is hypnotic. It has volume; it carries. It tells us that he is secure, relaxed, friendly, sensuous.

Although Henry Kissinger and Roger Moore both have bass voices, they have different sounds. And the sound is the important thing. When Moore says "hello," his voice is a greeting. It welcomes us. When Kissinger says "hello," we nod off.

What does your voice say about you?

You probably already know if your voice is too high or too low. If you are not absolutely certain, that is the first thing to find out. *It is important that you move in the right direction.*

Direction is the key to a winning voice. Should you go higher or lower, softer or louder? That's all you need to know to start on the road to success. It is not necessary to spend weeks, months, even years turning a losing voice into a winner. You should find that voice in seconds. After that, it takes only minutes a day to maintain it.

Start by gently humming the first line of a simple tune, such as "Happy Birthday" or "Row, Row, Row Your Boat," keeping your lips closed. These are songs everyone knows, and their uncomplicated melodies will give your real voice a chance to come out.

A good, winning voice should come *naturally*. I stress the word "natural" because that element is essential if you are to find your true, winning voice. No matter how misused your voice is now, it is almost always possible for you to talk in a richer, fuller, more *natural* voice—one that has "star quality."

Hum "Happy Birthday" once more. *Hum*, don't sing. Few people can really sing, but we can all hum.

As you hummed, did you hear what happened to your voice? Did you feel it going down? Or rising? Your voice should move in whichever direction that is natural for you.

Try gently humming the melody again as you read on. Can you feel a balanced vibration around your nose and mouth, in the area known as the mask? You should. It is from there that a good voice is projected. The vibration tells you that the voice is placed correctly.

As you move through the pages of the book, you will learn how this simple exercise, and a few others, can give you a better, more effective voice. And it truly is as easy as one, two, three—proper pitch, balanced tone focus and midsection breath support.

A SOUND VOICE MAKES A SOUND IMPRESSION

Personal impression counts for everything. A strong statement, but true. We spend years educating our minds. We learn to dress and eat well. We try to take care of our bodies. We want to look good, not only for ourselves, but for others. We become *someone*, an individual with a very unique personal identity. We assume an image.

When you meet someone, it is important to make a strong, positive impression. In a face-to-face encounter, your voice is one of the first things the person notices about you. Over the telephone, it is the *only* thing.

Remember the Lina Lamont character in *Singin' In The Rain*, played by Jean Hagen? Lina was a glamorous movie star, the darling of the silent screen. But when sound came to movies, and Lina opened her mouth, everyone laughed. Lina's voice was exaggerated, but the point was not. The voice can work for or against you. It can make you or break you.

It's a fact of life that a poor sound makes a poor impression. No one likes to listen to a blah, wimpy, or whiny voice, or one that drags, cracks and goes haywire. Too many people today do not take the time to really talk. They speak in grunt language, garbling their sentences with words like "I mean" and "You know?"

Mumblers, grunters, and the like have a difficult time making a name for themselves because they are almost impossible to understand. They cannot express thoughts and ideas clearly. They are asked to repeat themselves. Their voices tire quickly. They aren't heard or listened to.

It takes a sound voice to command attention. Anyone who seeks authority has such a voice—executives, lawyers, teachers, actors, men and women in all occupations. The fact is, *everyone* has such a voice at his or her command, but most don't know how to use it.

A voice is like a diamond. If polished, it glows and attracts. But if it isn't polished, it is just another hidden gem.

VOICE LANGUAGE VS. BODY LANGUAGE

Mike Tyson, the heavyweight slugger, is a big bruiser. He speaks in a thin, light voice.

Suzanne Pleshette and Brenda Vaccaro are brilliant actresses and beautiful women. Their voices are gruff and unexpected. Like Mike Tyson , their voices do not match their appearances.

Donna is 34 years old. She works in an advertising agency. "Do something about my voice," she pleaded not long ago. "It's not getting me anywhere. I sound like a kid."

Marie has a daughter in junior high school. Whenever she answers the phone she is mistaken for her youngster.

Bert sells printing supplies. His career is suffering, he complains, because of his voice. He has been told that he sounds weak and uncertain.

There are thousands of stories about people who look great but have poor voices. Poor for them, that is, because their voices are too high or too low, too weak or too gruff. A man should not sound wimpy. A man or woman of any age, particularly if he or she is seeking success, should not sound like a child—or the opposite sex.

Beautiful clothes and perfect stature cannot mask a poor voice. Once the mouth opens, the illusion is shattered.

For most people, the problem starts when they are growing up. Their bodies mature but their voices do not. They simply go on speaking as they always have, believing that is the way they were meant to sound. Then comes the realization that their voices are holding them back.

If this scenario sounds familiar, do not despair. There is nothing really wrong with your voice. You just don't know how to use it.

Your voice is waiting to be helped. It has "star quality" capability, but without training, it will continue to deprive you of your real potential.

You may have already discovered your natural, winning voice by humming "Happy Birthday." Before we go on, hum the melody once again.

As you hummed, were you aware of the slight balanced vibration around your nose and mouth, in the mask area? The "buzz" indicates that you are right on target.

Here is another simple exercise that will help you locate your winning voice.

Say "um-hmm" with your lips closed, as if you are casually responding to a friend in conversation. Repeat several times. "Um-hmm ... um-hmm."

Listen to the sound of your "um-hmm" on a tape recorder. (Always keep a recorder handy to monitor your progress while doing the exercises.) If your voice is normally too low, the "um-hmm" will usually bring it up. Your voice should sound *naturally* higher, richer and fuller, even at this early stage. If your voice is normally too high, energizing your voice with "buzz words" and the Cooper Instant Voice Press should make it *naturally* lower, as I explain later.

HOW TO PUT PIZAZZ IN YOUR VOICE

There is an old saying in management that goes, "If you want to get something done, give it to a busy person." Whoever came up with that saying knew what they were talking about. Busy people do accomplish more. Work stimulates them. They seem more interesting, livelier.

Energy attracts.

It's the same with voices. A voice without energy is dull. It has dark, heavy tones that puts people to sleep, and makes others want to avoid you. A voice that is light and airy will also put people to sleep, because it lacks energy.

Too many people sound older than they are because their voices lack energy, or pizazz. Talk to them by phone and you imagine they are of an older generation. Meet them directly and you discover they are younger than you had envisioned.

The voice is like a camera; it has to be focused to work properly. When a camera is out of focus, the picture is off. When a voice is out of focus, the sound is off. A poorly focused voice can result in nasality, hoarseness, laryngitis, aches and pains in the throat, and difficulty being heard. The voice fades, breaks, or even gives out altogether. A properly focused voice blends resonance or sound from the mouth and the nose to create a dynamic, winning voice.

When the voice is poorly focused, its energy level is sharply curtailed. It is often necessary to push or force the words, which can be fatiguing. When it is properly focused, the voice comes out easily and with energy. Talking should be effortless; it is one of the pleasures of life. But how many people can honestly say that after speaking continuously?

Lack of energy in the voice results in a thin, weak sound. Unfortunately, the vast majority of Americans speak too softly. Of the countless voices I've heard over the years, most lacked life and energy. I estimate a high percentage of our society is afraid of speaking up and out. We are a land of muted talkers. No one wants to be a loud mouth. And so voices drift up and away—lighter than air, garbled, unheard and unappreciated, or they drop down, becoming muffled and guttural.

Voices that command attention have *P*izazz, are *O*pen and *W*inning. I like to think of them as *POW!* voices because they do not go unnoticed. They turn heads, win friends, and influence people.

How do you get a "POW!" voice? Not by turning up the volume. You don't have to force it; it should come naturally if you use your real, *natural* voice.

Hum the first line of "Happy Birthday" once again. Humming will almost always focus your voice, raising or lowering it to your natural level. Feel the buzz around your lips and nose? The balanced buzz tells you that your voice is coming out as it should—forward. If you speak from the mask area, your voice will no longer sound weak and thin. It will be stronger, clearer, and energized.

Try "um-hmm" again. Repeat. At first, you will hear the added power in your voice and think that you are speaking too loudly. Listen to yourself on a tape recorder. What you hear will surprise you.

You won't be a loud mouth, but you will have a voice with pizazz. You don't quite understand yet? Read on.

YOU KNOW YOUR BUSINESS— NOW SOUND LIKE IT

Helen's friends call her "lucky." She's bright, young, ambitious, and attractive. She has a responsible, good-paying position with a solid company. She wants to do even better, and she's working hard to make it happen.

Helen has it all, according to her friends. Helen isn't as sure. "I've had people tell me that my voice is my fortune," she said one day. "I've always been a good talker, but lately, I've been having trouble with my voice."

I could understand why. Helen was misusing her voice, speaking from deep in her throat. There was a time, not that many years ago, when women with low, throaty voices were thought to be assertive and seductive. (The movies glamorized the myth by casting actresses with low or husky voices in career women roles.) Today, the sound of such voices can signal voice trouble.

Helen isn't the only young executive to seek help in recent years. Hundreds of men and women have called or written to express their concerns and describe their symptoms. They tell of once strong voices now fading, frequent throat clearing, voices that tire or give out completely, and severe throat and neck pains.

Craig, an attorney, called in to a radio talk show I was doing. "I was in conference with a client today and my voice started giving out," he said. "It has happened before, but not this bad. I'm worried. Without my voice, I am lost in my work."

I asked Craig to hum "Happy Birthday" and he did. Then I asked him to say it, just the way he hummed it. Within seconds his voice sounded clearer, richer, and fuller. The raspiness disappeared. So did the panic and much of Craig's concern. He came in for a consultation and is now working on a series of exercises to keep his voice in strong, working condition.

There are high risk voices, just as there are high risk occupations. Teachers have them. So do executives, salesmen, ministers, lawyers, singers—anyone who talks for a living.

When you know your business, sound like you do. Don't let a poor or misused voice come between you and all you've worked so hard to achieve. A strong, confident, well-used voice won't guarantee success, but it is one of the best means of getting you there.

QUESTIONS & ANSWERS

Q: **Do people judge a person by his voice?**

A: Many people do. Ask them. They make snap judgments about a person simply from what they hear. Voice is thought to *reflect* a person's personality. That isn't always true because the person may not be using his or her voice correctly, not having had any direction. They may, in fact, be reflecting sounds from family and society. The well-used voice has a "feel- good" sound. It builds the speaker's confidence and makes a positive impression on others. A natural, healthy voice can turn lives around.

Q: **Can a good voice make you feel better?**

A: Definitely. It gives you assurance that you are "someone," that people are listening to you, not tuning you out. Have you ever noticed during a conversation that people may turn away, forget you, or even ignore you? That may be because your voice isn't representing you as best it can. It doesn't get the attention it, and you, deserve. Once you find your natural voice, you may feel better, be more effective, and be listened to.

Q: **What do you mean by pitch?**

A: The pitch of voice should be a range of notes centering around the natural or optimal pitch level that you should use when you speak.

Q: **What difference does a voice make to an executive?**

A: Not long ago, the president of a blue chip company spoke before a large group of employees. He sounded unenthusiastic and down. "The audience picked up on that," remarked a top company official. "The executive's voice can lead or deny leadership."

During his Administration, Ronald Reagan led the country with his style, his manner, and his voice. When Walter Mondale was running for president, he didn't gain too many ears. In my opinion, his voice had a great deal to do with it.

Q: Why is it that primarily performers—actors, singers, public speakers— work on their voices?

A: This is a voice myth. Henry Fonda was losing his voice when he came to me prior to filming *On Golden Pond*. I've worked with Anne Bancroft, Diahann Carroll, Richard Crenna, Joan Rivers, Cheryl Ladd, Rob Lowe and many other performers whose voices are their fortunes. But you don't have to be a star to sound like one. The majority of the people I see are not entertainers. They are people who need to communicate, at home and at work, in the kitchen or in the classroom, or at the conference table. In today's highly competitive world, the quality of your voice can have a bearing on the quality of your life.

The fact is, whenever you use your voice to communicate with another person you are speaking in public. That makes you "a public speaker." Shouldn't you put your best voice forward?

Q: Isn't it true that nobody really listens to your voice, only what you have to say?

A: This, again, is a voice myth. It is almost impossible to be successful today without an effective voice. Ask a personnel director. Your voice, and how you sound, could very well be the deciding factor in your landing a job. The words you use during an interview may be on target, strong and self- confident, but if they are said in a weak way, you might as well pick up your resume and go home. When trying to make an impression, words are often less important than the sound and tone you use when you say them.

Q: My friends tell me that you can talk your way to success. Is that true?

A: People have been doing that for ages, and they will continue to do so for all time. Talking is one of humankind's basic means of communication. He who knows how to talk—and can talk well—can talk his way to success. There is nothing new, or old, about it. It is just a fact of life.

Q: I have strained my voice. My friends have told me not to talk louder than a whisper or else I will strain it further. What do you think?

A: That is a common belief but, in fact, is not true. It's easy enough to talk softly, but then you are not yourself, and you are not using your real voice. More often than not, if you continue whispering or talking softly, you wind up with a serious voice disorder. First, you need to have your throat checked by a doctor. Then you need to learn how to speak properly, and with as much volume and ease as you want. It can be done. In fact, people who were once advised as you were, cannot believe that they ever considered such a myth.

Q: Why should I work on my speaking voice? Isn't it the one I was born with?

A: This is a voice myth. We are all creatures of habit. We get into a voice pattern and stay with it, believing that it is our only option. It is not. I can't put a voice in you, but I can show you how to bring out your God-given *natural* voice, one that has star quality. You can have a voice that is richer, fuller, and easier to listen to.

Chapter 2

Finding Your Winning Voice–in Seconds

THE HUMMING OF AMERICA

Humming is as natural as breathing. Many people enjoy humming. Frank Sinatra is said to hum to warm up his voice. The noted poet William Butler Yeats hummed while writing poems. Constantin Stanislavski, the legendary acting coach, talked about how humming could produce the feel for the right voice.

Have you noticed that your voice changes when you hum? Your humming voice is different from your speaking voice. It's richer, fuller, stronger. Humming can bring out your *natural* voice.

Humming often is your vocal "private eye," your built-in radar system to help you locate your true, normal speaking voice. It guides you without special equipment or expense. You have everything you need to make it work.

If you are serious about improving your voice, and yourself, start by humming. There's no easier, more effective way.

Earlier, you began by humming the first line of "Happy Birthday." Hum the tune again now.

Did you feel a slight vibration around your nose and lips, in the mask area? As I stated before, talking in the mask is essential to having a stronger, more effective, *winning* voice.

Once again, hum "Happy Birthday."

Feel the "buzz"? This can indicate natural tone focus and pitch for your voice. Now, rather than humming just the melody to "Happy Birthday," hum the words to yourself with your lips closed. Repeat only the first two phrases, alternating humming and saying the words aloud. "Hum-happy- hum-birthday-hum-to-hum-you, hum-happy-hum-birthday-hum-to-hum- you."

Finally, keep the same voice level and just say the words to the first two phrases.

Another simple tune to use to help focus your voice is the first phrase of "Row, Row, Row Your Boat." First hum the phrase. Then put words between each "hum." Finally, say the words aloud, energizing your voice as you speak.

A famous British actor once asked me, "Where should your tongue be when you hum?"

Until then, I hadn't thought about the position of the tongue. "Where do you place yours?" I asked.

"Against the roof of my mouth," he replied.

I tried it his way, and felt the same buzz in the mask that I did when my tongue was flat. But I liked the tongue flat rather than up. Keeping my tongue on the bottom of my mouth seemed to allow the sound to come forward better.

Actually, the placement of the tongue is not that crucial. It is the focused humming that's important. And that is what I stress to new patients or anyone who is interested in a better, more effective voice.

Several times a week, I appear on radio talk shows where I answer questions from callers who are concerned about their voices. Before I offer advice, I often ask a caller to hum the first line of "Happy Birthday" or "Row, Row, Row Your Boat." Even over the telephone, it is easy to hear the difference between their speaking voices and humming voices. Humming is the most basic of all voice exercises, and the fastest way to find one's natural voice. That is, the natural, God-given voice.

Once you have found yours, don't stop humming. Hum the words of your newspaper each morning to relax your "morning voice" while raising or lowering the pitch to your natural level.

(Johnny Carson, a great talker, has what I call the "morning voice"; he calls it the grumpies.) Hum the words of a book or memo from time to time during the day. Hum the names on street signs as you drive along. Hum the names of products as you scan the shelves in your market. As you think to yourself, hum your thoughts. Hum whenever you can.

Humming can revitalize an older voice and make it sound young again. Humming can help make a "kid" voice sound adult. Humming is a key to unlocking the voice that can lead you to greater success.

UM-HMM: YOUR PUBLIC 'HMMM'

Say "um-hmm," as if you are responding to someone in conversation. Keep your lips together and try not to force the sound. Be as spontaneous and sincere as possible.

"Um-hmm."

Again.

"Um-hmm."

Say "um-hmm" once more, then follow with "one."

"Um-hmm ... one."

Could you hear the difference in your voice when you said "um-hmm" and "one"? For most people, there is a noticeable difference. Because while "um-hmm" tends to bring out your new, natural voice, the number was probably spoken in your old voice. Try it again, keeping the "um-hmm" and the number at the same pitch level and tone focus.

Could you feel the sound vibrating around your nose and mouth when you said "um-hmm"? The "buzz" is telling you where your voice should be placed, and the tone you should use. It may also be telling you that the voice you have been using for so long is not really "yours" at all, at least, not the natural voice you believed it to be.

Let's talk about the buzz or vibration. The area around the lips and nose is called the mask. (See Diagram A.) This term comes from ancient Greek times when male actors literally spoke through a mask when portraying women, since women were not allowed on stage.

To begin with, the throat or pharynx extends from your eyebrows to your voice box, located at the fifth and sixth vertebrae of the neck. (There are seven vertebra in the neck.) Basically, your throat

The Mask

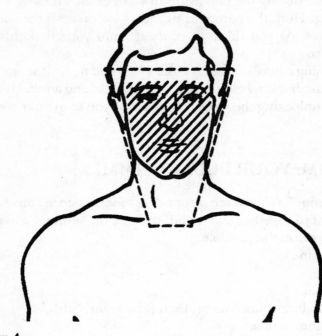

Diagram A

can be divided into three resonance zones, the lower or laryngo-pharynx area (the voice box), the middle or oro-pharynx area (the mouth), and the upper or naso-pharynx area (the nose).

The throat is shaped like a megaphone, the narrow portion beginning at the voice box and widening as it moves upward to the eyebrows. **(See Diagram B.)** The basic sound of the voice is produced at the vocal cords. This sound is very light. The amplification of this sound is produced in the mask (around the lips and nose) or as I term it, the two-thirds solution, referring to the upper two resonance areas. All good or great voices are focused in the two- thirds solution area. The blend of oral and nasal resonance is what creates the vibration in the two-thirds mask area and makes for an efficient and aesthetic voice. This resonance must be blended. Nasal resonance is a key element in making the voice alive and well. Too much nasal resonance makes the voice nasal sounding. **(See Diagram B—tip of**

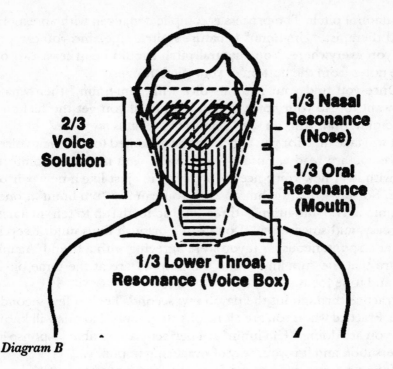

1/3 Nasal
Resonance
(Nose)

2/3
Voice
Solution

1/3 Oral
Resonance
(Mouth)

1/3 Lower Throat
Resonance (Voice Box)

Diagram B

nasal area.) The fear of nasal resonance causes many people to use lower throat resonance. Forced lower throat resonance causes voice problems, including tired voice, hoarseness, lack of carrying power, and other negatives associated with a wrong voice. (**See Diagram B— lower throat area.**)

Mask resonance is not only the key to a winning voice, but also voice health and longevity of voice. It provides carrying power, strength, and durability of tone. It gives you everything you ever wanted in your voice and more. Balanced resonance allows you to project your voice with more or less volume, with ease and comfort. This is the technique good public speakers and talented actors rely on when on stage without a microphone.

Now, let's get back to locating your voice. Like humming, "um-hmm," helps you find your natural voice in seconds. In the past, it was necessary to work with a piano, using musical scales. The problem with that method, aside from needing special equipment, was someone had to go up and down the keyboard with you and identify your natural pitch. The process is complicated, even with an experienced therapist. "Um-hmm" is nature's pitch pipe, and you carry it with you everywhere. Your natural pitch should be at least two or three notes from the bottom of your pitch range.

Once you find your natural voice with "um-hmm," then what? You want to use your voice at that level until you get the feel and sound of it, until you can say, "That is me. That is *my* voice."

It will take time for you to become accustomed to your new voice. Before you are ready to use it—*really* use it—you must feel comfortable with it. A new voice needs "breaking in" just like a new pair of shoes. So stay with "um-hmm" until you can say "um-hmm ... one, um-hmm ... two, um-hmm ... three" and so forth (up to ten) in a natural, easy, and sincere way. Don't force or push the sound. Keep it light and spontaneous, as if you were agreeing with a friend. Again, be sure that the "um-hmm" and the number are at the same pitch level and tone focus.

Practice throughout the day, a few seconds here, a few seconds there. Practice when you are alone or with people. No one will know what you are doing. "Um-hmm" is a perfectly acceptable response in conversation and it is your way of practicing in public.

Your next step is to move from the "um-hmm" to just "hmm," which can be used during your private practice moments. "Hmm" is a basically well- focused and balanced tone incorporating oral and nasal resonance, and gives you the feeling of a natural and focused voice.

Now try "hmm-one," "hmm-two," "hmm-three." If you energize the "hmm," you will get a tingle around the lips and the nose, or mask area. Be sure that the number is at the same pitch level and tone focus as the "hmm."

THE COOPER INSTANT VOICE PRESS

Have you been able to locate your natural pitch by using the humming or "um-hmm" method? Your *natural* pitch is your optimal pitch, and it is most likely different from your *habitual* pitch.

Test yourself once more. Hum the first line of "Happy Birthday." Now say "um-hmm ... one," "um-hmm ... two," "um-hmm ... three."

Did you feel a slight resonance around your nose and mouth as you did the exercises? The tingle tells you that you're placing your voice correctly.

Perhaps you still are not certain that you have found your natural pitch level and tone focus. An excellent backup exercise is the Cooper Instant Voice Press, which has been so successful that patients often refer to it as "pressing your magic button." **(See Diagram C)** The Instant Voice Press is a holistic technique that basically gives you the correct tone focus, natural pitch level and range, and the sound of your real voice. Contrary to prior techniques that worked with only one element at a time, this a simple 3-for-1 procedure that gives you "everything in a nutshell."

Begin by placing one hand on your solar plexus (the area at the bottom of the breast bone). Relax your stomach so that it moves in and out as you breathe. With your lips closed, hum while repeatedly pressing your solar plexus with your fingers in a light, quick fashion. "Hmmmm." (Hold that hum.) "Hmmmmmmmmmm." Because of the

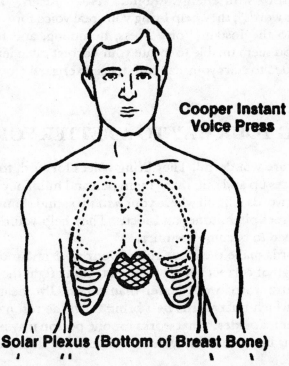

Cooper Instant Voice Press

Solar Plexus (Bottom of Breast Bone)

Diagram C

pressing, the "hmm" will actually break up into short bursts of sound like "hmm-hmm-hmm-hmm-hmm ...."

Do this exercise once again. Close your lips and hum while lightly pressing your fingers at the bottom of the breast bone, where the two sides of the rib cage join. As the sound escapes, you will feel a buzz around your mouth and nose. You are actually directing your voice into the mask area, precisely where it should be.

Next, do the Instant Voice Press with your mouth open, saying "Ahhhhh." I have used these techniques for years to help individuals find their real voices in seconds.

Next, try the exercise again, adding a number as you press. This should sound like "hmm-hmm-one," "hmm-hmm-two," "hmm-hmm-three." Then use "ah-ah-one," "ah-ah-two," "ah-ah-three."

Finally, carry this sound over to talking, beginning with one word at a time. "Ah-put-ah-the-ah-milk-ah-out." Keep the sentence short and learn to talk on the buzz.

Can you achieve that same pitch level without pressing your magic button? Raise both hands high above your head and repeat the following words with energy. "Right." "No." "Really." I call these words "buzz words"; they help bring your real voice forward.

Revert to the Instant Voice Press, humming, and buzz words whenever you seem unable to locate your correct pitch level. In fact, it's a good idea to start your day with these exercises.

BUZZING YOUR WAY TO A BETTER VOICE

Buzz words are wonderful. They bring voices forward, to the mask. They lift voices up and out, make them rich and full. They are energy words. Buzz words tell you where your *natural* sound should be. They indicate correct pitch, tone, and focus. They help you develop the voice you need to become a winner.

Buzz words make the area around your nose and mouth tingle, which is a sign of correct voice placement. Don't fight the sensation.

Some buzz words work better than others. I've heard patients argue over which buzz words best bring forth the resonance in the mask. I never take sides. What works for one person may not help another. So it is up to each individual to determine the most effective words to use.

Which buzz word works best for you? Is it "right"? Is it "really"? Is it "no"?

Here are others to try:

Hello	Do	Hey	Wow	Oh	Might
Ready	Great	Go	Show	Push	Be

Alternate these words from time to time as you perform the following exercises. While each of them helps to naturally bring your voice forward, to the mask, remember to speak them as if you *really* mean them. In other words, when you say "right," say it with conviction. *Right!*

Stand straight, with your hands stretched over your head.

Say "Oh!"

"Right!"

"Really!"

"Um-hmm."

Now, still standing, bend forward from the waist as far as you can. Let your head and arms dangle loosely. Then say buzz words followed by numbers. Keep in mind that the number should be at the same pitch level and tone focus as the buzz word.

Say "really!"

"Really ... one!"

"Really ... two!"

"Really ... three!"

"Really ... four!"

"Um-hmm."

Next, stand straight again. With your arms at your sides, say "right!"

Say "hello!"

"Really!"

"Ready!"

"Um-hmm."

Relax.

As you performed the exercises, were you conscious of the resonance about your nose and mouth? With "the buzz" your voice should have taken on a new richness, clarity, and efficiency. It should have found its *natural sound*.

Are you ready to go one step farther? Stand with your arms at your sides and repeat the last exercise.

Say "right!"

"Hello!"

"Really!"

"Um-hmm."

"Um-hmm-*my*-um-hmm-*name*-um-hmm-*is*-um-hmm-*your name*."

Did you feel the buzz? Did you hear your natural voice, the voice you can use all day without fatigue or hoarseness? If you didn't tape record yourself during the exercise, do it now; then listen to the play-back. If your voice was too high, it should have come down. If too low, it should have risen. The change may only be subtle, but you will notice a difference—a positive difference. You can have a dynamic new sound that can lead to winning ways. You may find you are heard, listened to, liked, desired by the opposite sex, and can land that job you've been seeking.

With a little practice, your dynamic new, winning sound can become habitually yours.

THE VOICE MIRROR MACHINE

Patients will occasionally tell me that they have trouble practicing. The exercises are simple enough, they say, but "other factors" seem to inhibit them. Some people admit feeling uncomfortable practicing at home because of distractions. Others simply are unsure of themselves. They have hummed, "um-hmmed," tried the Cooper Instant Voice Press and said the buzz words. They hear a new sound, but they cannot believe that it is really theirs. Making the transition from their old, habitual voice to their natural pitch level and balanced tone focus becomes an unsettling experience.

A talk show hostess came to my office not long ago. Her voice was failing and she didn't know why. She had seen a medical doctor, who prescribed medication and rest, but her condition was worsening. She feared her career was in jeopardy.

The young lady talked for a living. As a popular Hollywood resident, she was frequently seen on the town, attending various business functions and social gatherings. Occasionally, she hosted all night telethons and, whenever possible, she rooted for her favorite sports team. She was constantly using her voice, often forcing it to be heard above the crowd.

Talking continually is fine. Talking *wrong* continually is not.

With the failure of her voice came emotional stress and strain. She let her feelings dictate her pitch level. She spoke low, and from down in the throat.

"Your voice will come back once you get it out of your lower throat," I told her. "It is essential you keep your pitch *up*." She hummed for me, then practiced the buzz words. She could feel the tingle around her nose and mouth, and hear the difference in her voice. It sounded normal, natural, and healthy.

She was thrilled to have her proper voice back again, and so easily. But now she was concerned she might lose it as quickly as she had found it.

"Not as long as you talk at the same pitch level where you hum," I said. "Let your hum be your guide. Go under it and you'll wind up in the lower throat, your danger zone. The key is to speak in the tone of your hum, or 'um- hmm,' then carry the tone focus into conversation."

"And how do I do that?" she asked.

"By practicing."

She was back in the office a few days later. "I can't do it at home," she said. "I can't even exercise at home. I have to go to a gym."

I led her into a practice room and sat her before a small device often used for office therapy, called a Voice Mirror Machine. About the size of a 19 inch monitor, two columns of lights marked with the corresponding musical notes blink on and off in response to the patient's speaking or humming. By showing the patient's pitch level in lights, this instrument provides immediate visual feedback for proper voice placement. (I direct the patient to the correct pitch level and contrast it with the old pitch level.)

I asked her to hum the first line of "Happy Birthday" and watch as the lights flickered on the screen. "Now I can *hear and see* where my voice should be placed," she said. The lights made practicing easier for her.

I cautioned her, then, against relying too heavily on the Voice Mirror Machine. Soon she would have to learn to place her voice correctly on her own, since she wouldn't always have the device. "Check the lights to make sure you stay within your natural range," I told her. "At the same time, be conscious of the buzz around your nose and lips. Always go for the buzz."

In a different atmosphere, working with the machine, the talk show hostess was suddenly able to practice. She hummed "Happy Birthday" again, and said the buzz words. She then began the following series of voice exercises created specifically for people who talk too low in pitch.

These exercises can be used anywhere. But, they are recommended *only* if your voice is focused in your lower throat, not if you have a sound that is too high or nasal. If you are talking from the lower throat, and your hum indicates that your pitch should be raised, include these exercises in your daily practice routine.

Start by saying "zim-zim."

Repeat. "Zim-zim."

Do you feel the buzz in the mask area, that is, around your nose and mouth? The buzz is nature's guiding light. It tells you when you have the correct tone and focus. Make sure you feel the buzz before you proceed.

Repeat "zim-zim." Then "zim-zim ... one, zim-zim ... two, zim-zim ... three" on up to ten, maintaining the same pitch and focus.

The following is what I call the Cooper Vowel Chart. It is a unique system that will help you correctly place your voice in the mask area, around the nose and lips. Locate your correct vowel group and begin the exercise.

The vowels listed under Group I are for voices that are too low, too far down in the throat. Those in Group II and Group III should be used only if your voice is too high and thin. With each vowel, count from one to ten, remembering to keep the same pitch and tone focus on the numbers as you use on the vowels. Put energy in your voice as you practice.

COOPER VOWEL CHART

Group 1	Group 2	Group 3
Me-Me	Mo-Mo	Mu-Mu
Ne-Ne	No-No	Nu-Nu
Ze-Ze	Zo-Zo	Zu-Zu
Zim-Zim	Za-Za	Ma-Ma

GETTING INTO THE RIGHT VOICE

Before you try conversation, test your new voice at home with the following sentences. They contain non-emotional, non-threatening words to bring your new voice forward. Feel for the all-important buzz around your lips and nose as you speak. (Practice the first few sentences until you feel comfortable with them, then practice a few more. Repeat before moving on.)

As you proceed with the practice sentences, monitor yourself before each one with a casual and sincere "um-hmm," which can help you readily re-establish proper pitch level and tone focus. "Um-hmm" whenever you feel it is necessary. Keep in mind that it can be between sentences or between words within the sentences.

Say "um-hmm." Feel the buzz, then continue to talk at that level.

These sentences can be helpful if you are too high in pitch:

1. The law saw him withdraw from fiction to reality.
2. He drew a claw with a hacksaw and it was without a flaw.
3. A mall is not a hall, but a hall may become a mall.
4. A man with a horn is like a writer who has found his form.
5. He had corn in the morning, and prawns for lunch, and at evening he crawled and sprawled on the lawn while he talked about the raucous bunch.
6. She was enthralled by the shawl he bought for her stall, until she found it was neither too tall nor too small.
7. What one ought often do, one almost always seldom does.
8. We are all always ready for awful awesome events, but seldom prepared for simple awkward situations.
9. Words such as "all, always, also, almost, already, often, awful" and such are almost always too all inclusive in meaning.
10. All is not what it appears to be because we often ought disguise the core of the matter.

These sentences can be helpful if you are too low in pitch:

1. The bright light had a light that could shine through the night.
2. The butterfly asked why while quite on high, and in the rain was still quite dry, as it did fly and went bye-bye.
3. Be you, be me, whomever you be, be happy.
4. He said that three and three must equal be.
5. The peak seemed to lean toward the deep reach of leaves.
6. He who eats as a treat may find himself heavy upon his feet.

7. Dream and you dream alone; scream and you scream alone; lean upon a team and you are better for that scheme.

8. The soil was a foil like his voice was a coil.

9. The mouse was in town, down in the ground building his house.

10. He had a gray sleigh that was sprayed with clay as he played.

GETTING INTO CONVERSATION

Through repetition of the voice exercises and practice sentences, you've familiarized yourself with various ways to locate your correct pitch and tone focus. You may even have tested your new sound in conversations with friends by sprinkling your responses with spontaneous and sincere "um- hmms" or buzz words.

It's possible, and quite understandable, that you may be hesitant to say more than "um-hmm" during this period of discovery. You wonder how your friends will react to your new voice. You're not quite sure of it yourself. Does it sound phony?

That's a natural concern. After all, you've been speaking in your old voice for many years. Getting away from it may be a little difficult, but no more so than breaking any bad habit.

How do you make the transition to using your dynamic new voice in conversation? You ease into it slowly, starting with an "um-hmm" response and following with an occasional buzz word, such as "right" or "really," whichever seems appropriate. Let the buzz words be your guide. They will help you carry your natural pitch and tone focus into conversation.

Should you feel yourself slipping back into your old, habitual voice, stop momentarily and "um-hmm." The slight pause as you talk will be barely noticeable, and it will get you back on the right track. And your frequent "um-hmms" as you respond to the other person should keep you there. This technique will be helpful as you use your new voice in conversation.

PRACTICE MAKES IT HAPPEN

You can find your natural voice in seconds, but it takes practice to keep it.

Practice is not something you *have* to do; you do it because you want to improve your voice. Only by practicing can you learn to identify, locate, and establish the right voice, the one you want to represent you.

"Um-hmm ... one." "Um-hmm ... two." "Um-hmm ... three."

"Hmm-one." "Hmm-two." "Hmm-three."

Contrary to popular opinion, practice does not always make perfect. Wrong practice leads to wrong results or what is known as "permanent wrong." Right practice, however, makes "permanent right."

How do you know if you are practicing correctly? Let the buzz words, the "um-hmm," or the Instant Voice Press be your guide.

When you do the exercises, do you feel a slight resonance or tingle around your nose and lips? You should if you are doing the exercises right.

Don't try to force or push the buzz. You'll only create an unnatural resonance. What you want is an easy, *natural* resonance, with a soft ring or buzz to it. You can feel the buzz slightly when you exercise correctly.

Place the finger of one hand on the bridge of your nose and the other hand lightly over your lips. Now hum the first line of "Happy Birthday" or "Row, Row, Row Your Boat." A soft resonance should be barely discernible.

Next, take one hand and place it lightly over your Adam's apple. Hum the tune again. Do you feel a slight vibration there, as well as around your nose and mouth? The buzz should not be stronger in any one area, but should be evenly distributed.

As I mentioned earlier, to make sure you are getting the right sound in your voice, you should practice as much as possible throughout the day. Constant repetition of the exercises is part of your retraining, as it reinforces the proper pitch level and tone focus. In other words, the more you practice, the faster your new voice will become natural to you, if you are practicing correctly.

Start by practicing 5 minutes a day. You needn't practice all five minutes at one time—30 seconds here, 30 seconds there will suffice, as long as you practice each hour. Later, as you become more voice-conscious and tuned into your proper voice level, you can eliminate some practice time. By then, however, you should be using your new voice in public.

Practicing in public should help speed your improvement. You can easily practice while among others by responding spontaneously with "um-hmm," since it is an acceptable response in conversation whether you are talking with someone in person or over the telephone. When alone, remember you can focus your voice with a simple "hmm" in the mask, spoken in a brief rat-a-tat manner.

Although the exercises are simple, you may find it difficult to stay with a regular practice routine, especially at the start. It might be helpful for you to work with a friend or colleague from time to time. You will, of course, have your tape recorder handy (always consider that as an invaluable partner), but you may feel the need for direct encouragement and reinforcement in order to reach your goal. A family member or a close friend can provide emotional support, if necessary, while helping to monitor your progress.

Are you maintaining your correct voice level? Are you moving too quickly or too slowly, accomplishing as much as you'd like or too little? Is your humming spontaneous or forced? Having someone around to answer your questions and offer suggestions often makes practicing easier. It's also nice to be able to share a feeling of accomplishment as your voice becomes richer, fuller, and stronger.

If you still have difficulty finding your new voice, I would suggest you seek help from a professional voice therapist, preferably one trained in the Cooper voice method. But, if you have continued hoarseness or any persistent voice problem, see a physician. Be aware that serious voice problems (growths, spastic dysphonia, paralyzed vocal cord, etc.) also require professional help.

Practicing your new voice is up to you. It's not enough to simply run through the exercises each day. You must follow the simple guidelines and practice correctly. Only right practice makes "permanent right."

"Um-hmm ... one." "Um-hmm ... two." "Um-hmm ... three." "Hmm-one." "Hmm-two." "Hmm-three." "Um-hmm ... *right*." Right!

QUESTIONS & ANSWERS

Q: Is it possible to have permanent laryngitis?

A: Some people think they do, and they think it is the way things have to be. But that's not necessarily true because permanent laryngitis doesn't exist ordinarily. If laryngitis or hoarseness lasts more than two weeks, the individual should see a medical doctor. So-called "permanent laryngitis" without medical cause merely indicates that you are hurting your voice by using it as you do. Nearly all the cases of "laryngitis" I have seen are not permanent at all. They are temporary, due to voice misuse and abuse. But continued wrong use of the voice creates a voice that leaves both patient and listener believing nothing can be done.

Q: I have been told to rest my voice, but I have to talk. What do I do?

A: You can talk all day long, under normal circumstances, if done correctly; your voice should go on and on, clearly and easily. There are exceptions, however. If you had surgery, you should rest your voice briefly—not long. If you yelled at a game and went hoarse, you should rest your voice. But if you are misusing your voice, resting it won't help. Once you start talking again, your voice will tire and continue to bother you. You need to learn how to use your voice properly.

Q: Talking is a major part of my job. I love to talk, but my voice tires easily. Is there something wrong with me? Some people can talk forever.

A: You don't know how to speak properly. You are using the wrong voice, either talking in the lower throat or too high in the throat. You must learn to balance the tone.

Q: My voice seems to get better as I lose weight. Is there any connection between the two?

A: The voice *may* be affected by being overweight. The body may tire, and anything that fatigues the body can affect the voice. Generally, the pitch becomes lower. It is much easier to speak lower as you become fatigued by the excess weight. Breathing becomes harder, so you work harder for breath support—and at the wrong pitch. Though being overweight can induce a voice problem, or add to it, the weight need not cause or contribute to voice difficulty. It depends upon the individual, the circumstances, and how the voice is used. Weight is but one factor that affects the voice.

Q: I have been told that my posture is the reason I have a bad voice. Is there any truth to that?

A: Posture has very little to do with voice production. The way you move your head, stand, or sit, is of little importance in the correct use of your voice. If you have a bad voice, it is due to incorrect pitch, tone focus, volume, quality, and breathing.

Q: My voice seems to be worse with a change in the weather. What is the connection?

A: Your emotions, most likely. If you are depressed or morose, the pitch and tone of voice may drop. If you are happy, the voice may rise. However, some people suffering from allergies are indeed affected by the weather. The voice mechanism may react to the pollens and become contained or falter. It needn't.

Q: My voice is always tender. I mean, it isn't very loud and it isn't heard very easily. It has always been that way. Is this natural and normal?

A: The tender voice is neither natural nor normal. It simply indicates that you are using your voice improperly. The natural voice has life, volume, and range. The abnormal voice has what you call a "tender" sound and feeling. The answer is to learn to use your voice naturally.

Q: I'm a 19-year-old guy with two voices. I have a very high voice, and a low voice. When I speak I never know which voice will pop out. What is happening to me? Can I do anything about it? It isn't very funny anymore.

A: You are between your old and new voices. Puberty and the change in body and mental structure have played havoc with your voice. Your high-pitched, falsetto voice is your old, established voice. The new, low-pitched voice is more your natural voice. It is essential you learn how to control the new voice, which pops into your speech now and then, and interrupts the high, falsetto voice you are still using. You are ready and able to use the new voice. Try it. Pitch your voice down, and let it stay low for a few weeks. The exercises in this book will help you.

Q: **Why don't I have a loud voice anymore? I try to shout but no one hears me.**

A: You did a little too much talking, in the wrong way. After you have abused your voice, your ability to make it louder is noticeably diminished. You might be arriving at a point where your vocal muscles have about taken all the punishment they can endure. The voice shows it's in trouble by its inability to be loud, or have any kind of normal or acceptable type of volume.

Q: **I know I have misused my voice for years. If I get my natural voice, will it stay with me?**

A: If you learn how to use your voice well, it should get stronger, bigger, and better. Keep this in mind. Of a 1974 follow-up study involving 128 of my voice patients, 98% were rated excellent or good from three months to seven years after completing voice therapy. (My study was published in 1974 in the *Journal of Speech and Hearing Disorders*, an official journal of the American Speech-Language-Hearing Association.)

Chapter 3

The Great American Voice Diet

GETTING INTO VOICE TRAINING

In business, we are virtually nameless without a "calling card" to announce who and what we are. Your voice is also a "calling card." Don't you want it to represent you at your best?

It isn't enough to have a voice that simply transmits words. To make a name for yourself and improve your position in life, your voice should be distinctive, full, rich, and dynamic. It has to sound good to be heard, listened to, and liked. A good, winning sound transmits how you feel about yourself.

Most people have incredible voices—voices that are wonderfully appealing. But they don't use them because they don't know they have them.

Kevin has an incredible voice, but it took him some time to realize it. A struggling computer salesman, Kevin spent his mornings making calls and his afternoons at the local gym playing basketball. Nearing 30, he had an unpleasant sounding voice, whiny and nasal. "I've talked that way since I was born," he said one day. "Impossible," I told him. "No one is born with a voice like that."

Kevin first heard his natural voice at the gym. When another player fouled him, he let out a bellow. Suddenly, his voice was no longer whiny, but booming. The sound of Kevin's natural voice caught the other players by surprise; I told him, "Now that is your real voice." I helped Kevin develop and use what he calls his "basketball voice"; he sounds great now.

Successful people who use their voices for a living, even those in the public eye, were not born with the voices you hear. They were born with the *ability* to have good and great voices. They *learned* to use them. We all have the ability. It is God-given and natural. But you need direction, and a sense of how to make your voice work for you.

How do you know when it is time to get into voice training? Ask yourself these questions: Do I honestly like my voice? Do I become self-conscious when I hear the sound of my voice? Does my voice create a positive image for me? Does my voice tire or give out easily? Do people ask me to repeat myself? Is my voice holding me back?

Perhaps a good friend has remarked about your voice. A *good friend is more likely to comment, wanting to be helpful. Business associates and social acquaintances rarely bother. You are simply left to wonder about missed opportunities.*

If you honestly don't know, listen to yourself on a tape recorder. Do you like what you hear? Is it a voice that sounds warm, dynamic, inviting? Does it exude confidence? Is it a voice you would hire—a voice that makes you want to listen?

If your voice doesn't have a winning sound, don't despair. Such a voice can be yours, and sooner than you may realize.

THE TIME FACTOR

One of the first questions new patients ask is, "How long will it take to improve my voice?" I know what they want to hear, a sincere promise of "one or two lessons," even "overnight."

It seems that everyone is in a hurry these days. We've become accustomed to living in a world of instant coffee, fast food, and fast-forward movies. We're always on the lookout for quick and easy ways to get things done.

The truth is, it takes only *seconds* to find a better, more dynamic voice, and then only *minutes* a day to maintain it. It is easy to find your winning voice, but to make it habitual—that is, to speak naturally and spontaneously in your new voice—will take some work.

How long did it take you to learn to drive a car? Some people become expert after only a few lessons. Others take a few months, maybe longer.

How long does it take to travel from one side of the country to the other? Doesn't it depend on how you do it? If you fly in a jet, it takes only hours. If you go by bus, it takes days. In a car, making frequent stops, it can take a week or more. The time you spend getting there is entirely up to you.

It's the same with retraining the voice. You can do it quickly or slowly, it is your choice. Success, however, will depend on how carefully you follow the easy exercises outlined. Cooperation and determination are the real keys. You must be willing to break old habits and change your voice image. You must *want* to improve your voice, and enhance your career or social relationships.

The average person makes the transition in three to six months. With some people, a new, natural voice becomes automatic in one to three months. Some do it almost overnight. Most often, you are the key. (Patients with serious voice problems require longer periods of therapy.)

It's not realistic to set a time limitation for yourself since everyone progresses at a different rate. Just know that once you find your winning voice—and it can come almost instantaneously—it is yours to keep. But not without work, and a willingness to succeed.

THE SOUND OF YOUR NEW VOICE: THE VOICE IMAGE

Be prepared not to like your new voice at first. If you are like most people, it will sound and feel unnatural. But don't be discouraged. Stay with it, and soon it should begin to feel both natural and normal.

A major factor in changing from a wrong voice to a right voice is your voice image. The voice image is the way *you* hear yourself. It is the key psychological and emotional element as you find and use your new natural voice. Your old voice is part of you, and you have become so accustomed to it that any alteration may make you uncomfortable. The new voice may sound too loud, too full, too rich, and too different. If you ask others about your new voice, it is extremely credible and believable. You must discard your old voice image and establish and accept a new voice image based on your new natural voice.

Annie, a high school teacher from the Midwest, is a typical case in point. For years, she spoke softly. Her voice was dull, monotonous, without conviction and authority. It turned her students off, she said. No one paid attention to her.

Annie's new voice was well-modulated and strong, radiating self-confidence. She wasn't happy with it either. "It's not me," she remarked. "It doesn't *sound* like me."

"Is that why you don't like it?" I asked. "Or is it because you're not used to it?"

"Both," she answered quickly. Then, with some hesitation, she added, "I'm not quite sure. It's just ... so different."

Annie's voice *was* new and different. "You will have to use it for awhile before it feels normal to you," I told her.

"I don't think I can use it," she said. "It sounds strange. My students will laugh at me."

I asked Annie to make a recording of her new voice; then we played it back. "Tell me about your new voice now," I said.

Her face brightened. "It's really not as bad as I thought," she said. "To be honest, it's actually quite pleasant."

"Then you *do* like it?"

"Yes, I do. I really do. It's stronger, more outgoing and commanding."

"But it's not right for you?"

"It *is* right for me, except ...."

"Except what?"

"It sounds like somebody else."

"Who?"

"No one in particular. I'd just never know it was me."

I had to remind Annie about the purpose of her visit. "I thought you wanted to get away from your old sound."

"I did. I do."

"Then give yourself time. It won't be long before you will identify with your new voice." Everyone else would too, I told her, because her new voice—her natural, winning voice—revealed the *real* Annie, a woman people would like, listen to, and respect.

GETTING THE FEEL OF IT

It often takes me only a few seconds to discover what is wrong with a voice. Helping a person change takes longer.

Frank's old voice was gruff and throaty. After raising his pitch, his new voice came out clear and easy.

"It feels flaky," was his first comment. "I sound like a girl." To Frank, after hearing his gravelly voice for so many years, it probably did. To everyone else, it definitely did not.

Frank was so discouraged after hearing his new voice that he nearly gave up. But he was absolutely determined to improve his voice, and put an end to the nagging throat clearing that plagued him. "At first, speaking in my new voice wasn't easy," he admitted. "The hardest part was to use it without thinking." Now, he can. "Using the new pitch is like being reborn," he said recently. And his throat clearing has all but disappeared.

Ken found his new voice, then complained that he was going hoarse. "My old voice didn't make me hoarse," he said.

"You sound clear to me," I told him. He *was* clear.

"Well, it's hoarse," he countered. "It *feels* hoarse. I seem to have less power than before." To Ken, less power was equivalent to going hoarse.

I explained what was happening with his voice. Before, he was talking from the lower throat, pushing his voice out. Now, he talked from a different area, the mask. He didn't need to push his voice; it flowed easily and naturally. He would experience some discomfort for a time, caused by increased use of the muscles under the jaw and in the soft palate. But those symptoms would disappear with the consistent use of his proper and natural voice.

Unaccustomed to his new voice placement, Ken insisted, "I still feel hoarse."

I urged him to keep practicing, and he did. A few sessions later, he told me, "I really like the sound of my new voice. And, you know, it doesn't feel hoarse anymore."

I wasn't surprised.

Voices are like old shoes, comfortable and easy to slip into—even if they are not right for us, or cause problems, or hold us back. Your habitual voice has become such a part of you that subconsciously you may not want to part with it. And so you make up excuses, *anything* to delay the change.

Be patient with your new voice. *It is not your old voice.* Give your-self time and it should sound and feel natural to you. It should work for you, and pay big dividends. You can be the "someone" you've al-ways wanted to be. People may begin to respect and admire you, wondering what it is about you that makes them want to be with you. You can radiate energy and confidence. You can sound more dy-namic. Now, talking can be fun and exciting. Best of all, you can be the person you've always wanted to be.

PROMISE NOT TO BREATHE A WORD

There is one other factor, however, that you must master before the transition from your old, habitual voice to your new, natural voice can be successfully completed, and that is breathing properly.

You say you already know how to breathe? You simply draw in air and let it out. Right? Well, that's the basic idea. But what about your voice? Does your voice get enough air to support it? There is only one way to find out for certain. Try this easy test.

Sit up straight and hum "Happy Birthday" in an easy, casual way. "Hmm-hmm-hmm-hmm-hmm-hmm ...."

Were you aware of your breathing as you hummed? Not really? Then try one more exercise. Say "um-hmm" and count to five, pre-ceding each number with an "um-hmm."

"Um-hmm ... one."

"Um-hmm ... two."

"Um-hmm ... three."

Were you more aware of your breathing this time? Did your shoulders move up and down as you performed the exercise? Did your chest expand as you breathed in, and deflate as you spoke? If you noticed those things happening, you're like most everyone else.

"Chest out, stomach in!" Where have you heard *that* before? From your parents? From a gym teacher? From an army sergeant? A heaving chest was supposed to exercise the chest muscles and get more air into the lungs, which, in turn, made the blood richer and better. As a child, I was constantly reminded to stand straight with my chest out and stomach in. That was the secret to good posture, every-one told me. Almost all my female patients have told me their mothers instructed them to hold their stomachs in when they breathed. So all of these woman were using upper chest breathing, and it is the same for the men. You can have good posture and breathe correctly, without your stomach protruding. Good breathing is invisible to the eye.

The average person breathes eight to twelve times per minute, more if under stress. The chest cavity is heavy; it takes considerable effort to lift it up and out. Expanding the chest with every breath is not only pointless, it's exhausting.

Have you ever watched a sleeping person or animal breathe? Pets and people at rest breathe as nature intended, from the midsection. So, forget everything you've ever learned about chest breathing, and start breathing as nature intended.

When you use your midsection, or belly muscles, you relieve tension in the small, fragile muscles of the throat, allowing your voice to project more easily. Your stomach pumps the air up through your mouth and nose. **(See Diagram D)** The air reinforces the voice to make it richer, fuller, more resonant, and durable. Without air, we cannot talk.

People who have voice problems, especially severe voice problems such as spastic dysphonia or the "strangled voice" (see Chapter 9), reverse the breathing process. They push the stomach out as they talk instead of letting the stomach move in. Also they let the air out before they talk or as they start to talk. Then they are actually speaking without air or with only a minimal amount of reserve air. You can't drive a car on empty. Nor can you speak on empty, without air.

Almost every vocal coach and voice therapist knows you must use midsection breath support. Ask anyone who sings, acts, or uses the voice for a living. Many professionals in these fields will admit they have had voice problems at one time or another caused by improper breathing techniques. The voice demands air. Without enough air, you exhaust your body and foster a voice extremely limited in flexibility and listener appeal.

Breathing correctly from the midsection may be somewhat bothersome at first and, admittedly, a little tiring. But the muscles of the stomach adapt quickly, and once you learn to use them as nature intended, you'll find that you not only have more control of your voice, you'll feel better, too. In addition, using your stomach muscles can trim inches off your waist.

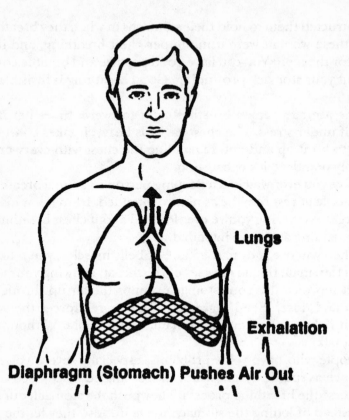

Diagram D

First you need to learn to breathe from your midsection. Sit on a chair with one hand on your chest and the other on your midsection. Breathe easily through your nostrils. Don't force the breathing or take a deep breath. You will find that your midsection moves out as you breathe in and that your chest remains stationary. If your chest is moving up as you breathe, you are breathing wrong for speech.

Another way of learning to breathe for speech is to lie flat on your back, nothing under your head, with one hand on your chest and one hand on your midsection. Relax and breathe in as though you are lying on the beach or in bed getting ready to go to sleep. Your midsection should move up, and the area of your waist should expand slightly. Your chest should not move. Practice breathing this

way until you become accustomed to the midsection as you breathe
through your nostrils. **(See Diagram E)** When you are comfortable
with midsection breathing, breathe in through your nostrils, but on
exhalation, purse your lips and blow out a steady stream of air. You
will feel the midsection move in gradually, smoothly, and progressively as you exhale the air. The next step is to breathe in with your
mouth slightly ajar. Exhale through the mouth. Be sure that as you
inhale, the chest does not raise. You will notice that your intake of
air is faster than your exhalation. Inhalation takes only a fraction of
a second, while exhalation may cover a period of 3 to 10 seconds.

When you have gained control of inhalation and exhalation in
the reclining position, follow the same procedure in a sitting position. Finally, practice in a standing position.

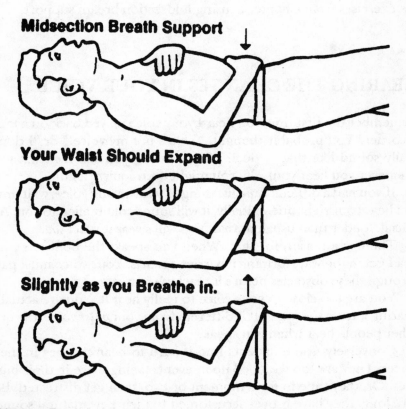

Midsection Breath Support

Your Waist Should Expand

Slightly as you Breathe in.

Diagram E

Now, breathe again. Now exhale slowly. Take another breath. As you let out the air, say "oh" or "ah." Feel the added energy air brings to your voice. The "um-hmm" and the "hmm" also help you to breathe correctly, from the midsection.

Everyone breathes at a different rate, but I like to take a breath every four or five seconds so there's enough air to support my voice when I speak. But I vary my breath intake as I talk, depending on the situation.

Once more, breathe from your midsection. Be sure to keep the stomach muscles relaxed. You can't breathe properly holding your stomach tightly in. The troubled voices around us prove that. America is a land of chest breathers, and poor voices. That fact is more than coincidental.

After you have learned midsection breath support, you must coordinate this with the correct pitch level and tone focus. Practice all the exercises from Chapter 2, using midsection breath support.

HEARING THE CHANGES IN YOUR VOICE

Remember the first time you heard your voice played back on a tape recorder? You probably thought, "That's not my voice!" or "I don't really sound like that ... do I?" Chances are you still feel that way whenever you hear yourself. You might even squirm a little.

If you had a difficult time listening to your wrong voice, wait until you hear your right one. Initially, it will sound totally alien to you. Artificial, louder than usual, unreal. You will swear it is *not you*.

There is a reason for that. When you speak, the bones in your head get in the way, forming a barrier of sorts. Your voice must pass through these obstacles before it reaches your ears.

You are too close to your voice to really hear it. You are actually hearing it from the *inside*. It is different from your *outer* voice, the one other people hear when you speak.

Conversely, some patients find it hard to hear changes in their voices. They are too wrapped up in events taking place in their busy lives. Or, they tune in for a moment or two, then get distracted. Before long, they have grown accustomed to their new, natural sound. For them, it has become normal.

Tobi did not recognize a change in her voice. A young professional, and a perfectionist, she began to question why she kept coming to see me, and what she was getting for her time and money. After listening to a playback of her "before" and "after" voices, she commented, "It's unbelievable. I'm really shocked to hear the difference between the two. I had no idea, the change has been so gradual."

Tobi needed to hear herself as others do. She stopped fighting and willingly continued her sessions to perfect subtle changes in her sound. "It works," she said, with new confidence. The young lady likes things that work.

If you are serious about upgrading your voice, it is important for you to hear yourself as others do. That's why I strongly recommend that you use a recording device when you practice the voice exercises, whether you are humming, using buzz words, the Cooper Instant Voice Press, or any of the other exercises. By taping your new voice, you should gain a truer sense of how you really sound, not how you *think* you sound. We hear ourselves through bone conduction, which is 3/1,000ths of a second faster than air conduction. The bones in our head distort sound. The tape recorder plays back what we actually sound like—and as others hear us—via air conduction.

Always keep a recorder handy. It will not only allow you to monitor your progress, it will help your voice retraining. The tapes help you honestly appraise the changes in your voice.

Hearing yourself will also dispel the sensation of loudness that you will surely experience with your new voice. You will discover that you are not shouting, or speaking any louder than you did in the past. It will simply sound that way to you because your voice has been correctly refocused to the mask area.

Once again, the sound you are hearing is all in your head. In time, and with practice, you should become comfortable with your new voice and develop a new voice image to go with it, a very positive reflection of yourself.

QUESTIONS & ANSWERS

Q: **Once my new voice becomes habitual, will I be able to use my old wrong voice?**

A: Your new voice should become so effective that you won't *want* to speak in your old voice. But if you really want your old voice back, just forget all you've learned about good voice production.

Q: **Do you really have to stop and breathe when speaking correctly?**

A: Yes, you do—but only temporarily, so no one notices it. Breathing is part of talking. You should breathe from the midsection every few seconds, maybe every four or five seconds at first. Later, when you master correct breathing, you can vary your intake.

Q: **For anyone with voice trouble, isn't it better to wait awhile to see if the problem clears itself?**

A: Waiting is not the answer. Troubled voices generally do not correct themselves. Waiting will only delay the retraining process and, in far too many cases, it worsens the problem. A proven way to correct many types of voice disorders is with voice rehabilitation.

Q: **A confidential voice is essential for me. As a teacher, I like to use such a voice in the classroom, and it seems to appeal to the students. But the voice does not carry, and it tires easily. What do you suggest?**

A: The confidential voice is one which affords intimacy to the listener, and allows you to keep your voice down. In some places it is an effective voice. But for the classroom where there are many students to be reached, it is necessary to alter this type of voice by slightly increasing volume. To do that you must have firm control of midsection breathing. You also need to raise your pitch somewhat, because the higher pitch carries better with less effort. Your voice will then be more effective in the classroom.

Q: **I frequently have a "frog" in my throat. What does that mean?**

A: Many allergists feel that a frog, or phlegm, is due to allergy problems, but my experience reveals it is a wrong voice more often than not. Talking too low or too high in pitch, and deep in the lower throat, can create phlegm, along with repeated throat clearing. There is a mucus gland right under the vocal cords, and when you squeeze the gland, which happens when you talk too low or too high in pitch or focus, mucus is released to protect the vocal cords. Talking at the right pitch and tone focus takes the pressure off the lower throat, and relieves throat clearing.

Q: Why are people surprised when I tell them I am training my speaking voice? Many people train the singing voice. My job requires a lot of talking and I want a good speaking voice. What is so strange about training it?

A: Nothing. People who react to you like that think the speaking voice cannot be changed or improved. You, however, have the good sense to realize how important your voice is to your career and to protect and improve it by seeking appropriate training. Essentially, the trained speaking voice is a fulfillment of your voice potential.

Q: Once I learn to breathe correctly from my midsection, will the technique remain with me?

A: Yes, unless you completely ignore what you have been taught. Under tension, or similar states, you might forget your training, or overlook it, but you will essentially retain your correct breathing pattern, if you learned it well in the beginning.

Q: Is it really necessary to listen to the replay of my voice as I practice voice exercises? Hearing myself makes me uncomfortable.

A: It is very important to listen to yourself in order to get acquainted with your real voice. To hear its tone, to accept it, like it—and then feel comfortable with it. At first, you don't even know your tone. The old pitch is more comfortable for you compared to the new pitch, and the old tone focus is more comfortable compared to the new one. But that is only for the present. The new tone focus and pitch range should save your voice and give you a permanent, durable, comfortable voice. It should remain clear and easy, and you can use it as you wish throughout the day.

Chapter 4

Why You Sound the Way You Do

WHY VOICES GO WRONG

Stan, a real estate salesman from the Midwest, came to see me last summer. He said he had an allergy that was affecting him both on the job and at home. He showed none of the usual signs of allergy, such as red, watery eyes and congestion, but he repeatedly cleared his throat as he talked. Stan's doctor told him that his nose was the problem, so he had surgery for a deviated septum. That, and three years of allergy shots, failed to help.

"Is it a virus?" Stan asked, clearing his throat once again.

"I think your problem is your voice," I said.

"My voice? Then why do I feel something in my lower throat, like a lump? And why do I get hoarse all the time?"

"Because you are talking incorrectly and you don't know it."

Stan had a voice that held to the bottom of his range. He was squeezing his voice out from his lower throat causing the throat clearing and hoarseness.

Another patient, Jenny, was an executive secretary. She came to me complaining about year-round sore throats, which she blamed on the ventilation system in her office: air conditioning in the summer and heat in the winter. Jenny sang in a choral group several nights a week. To protect her sore throat, Jenny's choir master told her to lower her pitch. So Jenny not only began singing but talking in a lower voice. Her throat continued to be sore, and grew hoarse.

When I told Jenny that she was practicing "voice abuse," she objected. It was a negative term, she said, implying intentional harm to oneself. She much preferred the word "misuse."

Whether you call it abuse or misuse, Stan and Jenny were unknowingly causing their own symptoms and problems. Fortunately, after instruction in the Cooper voice techniques, and practice, both overcame their voice problems and developed new, stronger voices.

Whatever you call it, the fact remains that the voice often is one of the most abused and misused functions of the human body. Millions of Americans suffer from laryngitis, hoarseness, throat clearing, coughing, tired, failing, and troubled voices. They don't realize that these symptoms may be caused by using the wrong voice.

Throat clearing is one of nature's most common ways of telling you something is wrong with your voice. Coughing is another. Your doctor may prescribe drugs to correct these symptoms, but are they listening to your voice?

A voice that is right may soon go wrong with too much alcohol. You become so relaxed that your voice drops down into your lower throat, the danger zone.

Laryngitis has many different causes, including smoking, the common cold, and various medical problems. When these problems are ruled out, the most common factors that create and prolong everyday laryngitis are vocal abuse and misuse.

If you suffer from laryngitis without medical cause, on a regular or continuing basis, you know that it does not go away easily. You have tried rest, pills, steam, gargles, shots, even vocal rest, and still it persists. Can anything be done? Yes, indeed.

You must learn to focus your voice with moderate volume. Do not try to compete with noise.

A common cold often lowers the voice pitch and brings it down to the lower throat. The tendency is for an individual to protect the voice by keeping the pitch down. Unfortunately, since that voice really isn't the natural or normal voice, the voice gets tired and hoarse, or it fails, creating laryngitis.

When a cold strikes, try to keep your "before the cold" voice going. If the pitch drops, bring it back up to your right pitch level and mask focus. The question is, how do you remember what your pitch level was before the cold started?

Use the exercises in Chapter 2 to relocate your correct pitch and tone focus. If you have any doubts use the Cooper Instant Voice Press with the "hmm- hmm-hmm" and the "ah-ah-ah."

Next time you have a cold, test your voice and your voice agility in this simple way. It should keep you talking, feeling better and doing better.

Our voices have a way of telling us when they are going wrong. Listen to the warning signals: the coughing, throat clearing, voice fatigue, and so on. If your voice sounds bad, it probably *is* bad and will not become better until you learn to talk correctly.

SYMPTOMS RELATED TO VOICE MISUSE

In my thirty years as a voice and speech pathologist, I have found that certain symptoms are related to the misuse and abuse of the speaking voice. I have all my patients fill out a Voice Evaluation Chart (see pages 48 and 49) which pinpoints negative sensory and auditory symptoms indicating a wrong voice. Here is a chance for you to evaluate your own voice. At the end of therapy, I have the patient fill out the form again. Also, I have my patients see a laryngologist for a laryngeal examination at the beginning of therapy, at the end of therapy, and as needed during the therapy process. The symptom sheet and the laryngeal examination allow me to follow the patient's progress, along with the playback of the new voice.

HOW TO FOCUS ON
YOUR NATURAL SOUND

The voice is like a camera; to work properly it has to be used in focus. When the voice is out of focus, the sound is off. Ears close, minds stray. Words drop dead in mid-air.

Most voices need to be refocused. Not knowing that can result in the negative auditory and sensory symptoms as noted in the Cooper Voice Evaluation Chart, shown on pages 48 and 49.

When the voice is out of focus, its energy level is sharply curtailed, so you have to push more to talk. That makes talking tiresome for you and puts a strain on your listeners. Talking should be effortless. It is one of the great pleasures of life, yet how many people can say that after talking for a time?

To find your natural sound, the voice must be focused in the mask, not in the vocal cords which produce a thin sound. People who squeeze their voice from the lower throat, wind up with troubled voices, and possibly more serious problems. When you talk with nasality these problems do not occur. You simply create "ear pollution."

It is so easy to focus your voice in the mask area by practicing the simple humming exercises, along with the Cooper Instant Voice Press. Focusing your voice may take only seconds, but learning to use your voice correctly in conversation takes time and practice. The effort will be worth it. Not only can you hear the difference between your old habitual voice and your new natural voice, you can *feel* it.

VOICE EVALUATION CHART

NAME_____DATE_____

SENSORY SYMPTOMS	ELIMINATED
___1. Non-productive throat clearing	_____
___2. Coughing	_____
___3. Progressive voice fatigue following brief or extended voice usage	_____
___4. Acute or chronic irritation or pain in or about the larynx or pharynx	_____
___5. Sternum pressure and/or pain	_____
___6. Neck muscle cording	_____
___7. Swelling of veins and/or arteries in the neck	_____
___8. Throat stiffness	_____
___9. Rapid voice fatigue	_____
__10. A feeling of a foreign substance or a "lump" in throat	_____
__11. Ear irritation, tickling or earache	_____
__12. Repeated sore throats	_____
__13. A tickling, tearing, soreness or burning sensation in the throat	_____
__14. Scratchy or dry throat	_____

__15. Tenderness of anterior and/or posterior
     strap muscles   _____

__16. Rumble in chest   _____

__17. Stinging sensation in soft palate   _____

__18. A feeling that talking is an effort   _____

__19. A choking feeling   _____

__20. Tension and/or tightness in the throat   _____

__21. Chronic toothache without apparent cause   _____

__22. Back neck tension   _____

__23. Headache   _____

__24. Mucus formation   _____

__25. Arytenoid tenderness   _____

__26. Trachael pressure   _____

__27. Anterior or posterior cervical pain   _____

__28. Pain at base of tongue   _____

AUDITORY SYMPTOMS

___1. Acute or chronic hoarseness   _____

___2. Reduced voice range   _____

___3. Inability to talk at will and at length in
     variable situations   _____

___4. Tone change from a clear voice to a breathy,
     raspy, squeaky, foggy, or rough voice   _____

___5. Repeated loss of voice   _____

___6. Laryngitis   _____

___7. Pitch too high; pitch too low   _____

___8. Voice too nasal; voice too throaty _____

___9. Voice comes and goes during the day or over
     a period of months   _____

__10. Clear voice in morning, tired/foggy voice later
     in day   _____

__11. Missed speech sounds   _____

YOUR NATURAL VOICE–IS IT REALLY YOU?

"I've talked like this all my life," I said, purposely exaggerating a high-pitched nasal twang. "It's hereditary. Everyone knows this is my natural voice. I just open my mouth and it comes out. Isn't that right?" I was speaking at a symposium of hospital administrators.

"I don't agree," a gentleman in the audience responded.

"Are you saying, sir, that you do more than open your mouth and talk? Do you really believe something else affects your voice?"

The man, who identified himself as Terry, paused for a moment before saying, "Your anatomical parts create the voice ... the sound."

"And the voice you are using is your real, or natural, voice?"

"I assume that's right."

I invited Terry to join me on the speaker's platform. I asked him to hold his hands above his head and say a few buzz words. Within minutes, Terry's voice had dropped in pitch. He had found his natural voice.

"Can you hear the difference?" I asked.

Terry nodded, and smiled sheepishly.

The people in the audience could hear Terry's new voice, too—his natural voice—and they liked what they heard. His new, natural voice was better than his old one: richer, fuller, and more confident.

Terry's old voice had a definite nasal resonance. A nasal voice is generally located too high in pitch, with excessive nasal resonance. (See Diagram F) Saying such buzz words as "right" and "no" with your hands raised above your head often will help lower your voice tone, making it richer and fuller, while softening, if not eliminating, the offensive nasal sound. You may not hear the changes in your head, but you should on a tape recording. Once you find your natural voice level, it is up to you to retain it by practicing the simple exercises.

Whether you are talking with people in person or on the phone, in business or social relationships, the right voice can help you lead a more productive life, and a healthier one, too. My files are filled with tapes of doctors, lawyers, teachers, executives, entertainers—people from all professions— who talked with a nasal voice because they believed that the voice they were using was the only voice they had.

Not all voices are as easy to correct as Terry's. Not long ago, a desperate young man came to see me after seeking medical help across the country. He'd had different kinds of checkups and speech therapy, without success. His voice was high-pitched, almost a falsetto, and was badly strained. For 20 years, Harold had been speaking incorrectly.

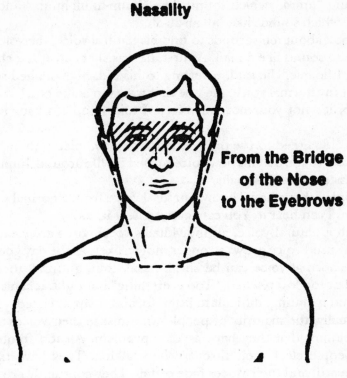

Nasality

**From the Bridge
of the Nose
to the Eyebrows**

Diagram F

Too often a doctor will look down your throat and take tests, but he may not be listening to your voice. So you go on talking as you do, complaining as you should, and getting worse.

"I can't go on like this," Harold told me. "Everyone makes fun of me. At times it gets so bad I want to kill myself."

I asked him to raise his hands above his head and say "no."

"No," he said in his weak voice.

"Say 'no' like you mean it."

"*No!*" His voice was lower, clearer and stronger.

"Say 'right'."

"*Right.*"

"Good. Now, lower your arms and press your 'magic button'."

"My what?"

I explained the Instant Voice Press to him, and he began humming while pushing lightly below his sternum in a staccato motion, first using "hmm," which sounds like "hmm-hmm-hmm," and then "ahhh," which sounds like "ah-ah-ah-ah."

It took about ten seconds to find his natural voice, the voice that made him sound like a man. At first, he was shocked at the change. "I sound hoarse," he said, reverting to his old, high-pitched sound. "It's not my normal voice, the one that wants to come out."

"No, it's not your normal voice," I told him, "it's your *natural* voice."

Harold agreed to use the new voice and completed therapy. He later wrote to me that his new voice turned his life around, improving it professionally and socially.

People ask me how I know a natural voice from a normal voice. I tell them I can hear it. You can learn to hear it, too.

With a natural voice, an individual's vocal cords are clear. The properly used voice grows stronger, not weaker, as the day goes on.

The normal voice can be shrill, nasal, thin, guttural, too high-pitched or too low-pitched. "Too everything" but right. It can also be harsh and irritating, difficult to listen to, and unappreciated.

Actually, the majority of people who misuse their voices are totally unaware that they have a voice problem. All too frequently, these people clear their throats when talking. They have trouble being heard, and their voices fade or fail. They constantly are asked to repeat themselves. And they experience neck aches and pains. These symptoms are signals of trouble ahead.

WE ALL HAVE "STAR-QUALITY" VOICES

"I hate my voice," Jennifer said, darkly. "It turns people off."

"Then why not change it?" I asked.

"Oh, I couldn't do that."

"Why not?"

"Because it wouldn't be *me* anymore."

"What do you mean?"

"If I didn't use *my* voice, my *real* voice, I'd sound very strange. No, worse than strange. Phony. Not like me, like somebody else."

"But you said you don't like your voice."

"I don't. No one does."

"Then do something about it. Change it."

"I can't," Jennifer said. "I don't want a new voice. I wouldn't like that either."

Jennifer wasn't the first person I had encountered who was put off by the suggestion of "a new voice." To her, like so many others, new meant artificial, unnatural. What she didn't realize was that the voice she had been using all along was artificial. She had never learned to let out the rich, beautiful voice that is within all of us.

There is a lot of emphasis today on being *natural*, yet so many people completely ignore their voices. They let them go unattended while they speak incorrectly, masking the God-given NATURAL sound that they could be using.

Almost all of us have potential star-quality voices—voices that are strong, full and effective. But too few of us use what we have because we don't realize it is there. From childhood on, we ignore our voices. We use voices that misrepresent us, and detract from who we really are. In other words, *your dynamic, natural voice is not speaking for you.*

Consider the time and money you have spent (and that was spent on you) over the years to develop your mind, your body, your appearance and talents. There were new clothes, books for school, perhaps braces, glasses or contact lenses, and lessons of one kind or another. Then you talk, and ruin it all.

Isn't it time to pay attention to your voice so that it may represent you both as you are and as you want to be?

Isn't it time to start developing your natural voice?

Your voice can be your fortune, yet you squander it away by using sounds that hurt you socially, professionally, and physically, as well.

The few seconds it takes to find your natural voice are worth spending. Raise your arms above your head and say the buzz words. Press your "magic button" (the Cooper Instant Voice Press). Then follow-up with the exercises discussed earlier to develop your natural sound. You can do them without anyone realizing it. Hum the first line of a simple tune when you are alone. (Caution: do not practice "humming along" to your favorite records or songs on the radio. The humming must be in your natural key, not that of the song being played.) When you are with people, respond with "um-hmm" whenever possible. No one will be offended. In fact, such a response is appreciated. It tells them you are listening to what they are saying. And remember, when you are alone, use a brief, sharp "hmm."

Why not practice this very moment? Hum the first line of "Happy Birthday" or "Row, Row, Row Your Boat." You might even hum the words in this book as you read along.

QUESTIONS & ANSWERS

Q: Is throat clearing emotional or is it a nervous habit?

A: Repeated throat clearing is often caused by poor voice habits. Nerves may trigger it initially, but are a minor cause compared to misuse of the voice.

Q: My husband has a poor voice, which limits him in his work. He won't seek help because he believes we are born with the voice we have—either a good voice or a bad voice. Is this true?

A: No, it's nonsense. We inherit only the basics. Some of us are naturals, but the rest of us learn poor pitch and tone focus from friends, relatives and society in general. In fact, almost everyone is born with the ability to have a star-quality voice. Genetically, physiologically, and psychologically the potential is there. Don't let wrong thinking limit your husband's chances for success.

Q: Why does it take so long to recover from a voice problem? I spent almost nine months trying to regain my voice. I must admit my voice was terrible and barely audible, but why nine months?

A: Few patients are referred to rehabilitation at the first signs of a voice disorder. The problem usually has gone on for many years, resulting in a long recovery period. It takes time, effort, and specific direction to overcome serious voice problems.

Q: My girlfriend has been complaining about her voice lately. She sings in a choir, and after practice her throat aches and her voice is hoarse. Should that happen?

A: No, not if the voice is used correctly. The symptoms you describe are caused by the wrong method of singing. Her larynx and throat, and subsequently her speaking voice, are showing the effects of the misuse of the singing voice. She should see a teacher of singing for proper training, so she can learn to sing without straining her voice.

Q: I am a teenager with a really nasal voice, like I talk through my nose. I hate the way I sound. It turns people off. What can I do?

A: You don't have to sound nasal when you talk. Nasality is simply a sound created by using your voice incorrectly. You need to cut down on the excessive nasal resonance by adding *oral* resonance to your voice. The steps to do this are outlined in this chapter and in Chapter 2.

Q: My voice is hoarse a good part of the day. I hardly raise it at all with the kids, but it is still hoarse. What should I do?

A: You are obviously misusing your voice pitch and tone focus. Somewhere along the line, you lost the placement of voice. It may have occurred overnight, so to speak, due to a cold or some incident, or it may have happened over a long period of time. Learn to use your natural voice. That means, learn to place your voice in the mask, where all good voices are placed.

Q: Do most patients accept that they have a voice problem that was created, and perpetuated, by voice misuse?

A: Rarely. Initially, most patients find it hard to believe that they have a voice disorder. They feel the voice is "normal," and that something else is causing the problem.

Q: Are voice difficulties universal?

A: Yes. The speaking voice often needs direction and training to develop its naturalness and beauty. There are influences everywhere, which deter it from becoming a natural, attractive voice.

Chapter 5

Voice Talk

IT'S THE VOICE THAT COUNTS

There is no avoiding the sound of a person's voice. You hear it and it influences your judgment. Something about it either attracts you or repels you.

When a voice is right, you want to hear more. When a voice is wrong, you want to cringe. That is not usually possible.

A beautiful voice can be mesmerizing. On the other hand, the most intellectual individual may be taken lightly, even ignored, if represented by a troubled or poor voice.

When Ron first came to my office he spoke very quickly, machine gun-style. His speech was clear one moment, muddled the next.

"People think I am drunk," Ron said with some clarity. He wasn't drunk, but he sounded that way. His words slurred. They came in great bursts, bunching together in unintelligible heaps.

Ron blamed his problem on an inferiority complex. Growing up, he was the youngest child in his family. When he talked, no one paid attention to him. He learned to talk fast so that he could get in everything he wanted to say.

As Ron's speech grew faster, his voice rose, along with his pitch. His voice became light and thin. He became what is known as a "mush-mouth speaker."

Ron now has a bass-baritone voice, which he found through the simple humming and "um-hmm" exercises. His new voice is his natural, true voice. It is rich, full, and strong. Ron likes his new voice, and so does everyone who hears it. People listen, and Ron can't believe his good fortune. He still rushes his words, but not as much as before, and he is learning to slow down.

Poor speech habits or patterns can lead to problem voices, and create problems for the individual. People who mumble, who talk in a monotone, whose voices are too high, too low, too thin or too nasal, generally turn off their listeners—no matter how knowledgeable they may be. Conversely, a beautiful voice can be hypnotic, even while reading the telephone book. A beautiful voice touches the head and the heart. It sells.

VOICE TYPES

The police have been using voice identification prints for years. A voice, like a fingerprint, is unique to every individual, which means that there are millions of voice sounds and combinations of sounds. However, despite all the combinations, all the variations, accents, twangs, and so on, I categorize two principle voice types: covert and overt.

Virtually everyone knows the comedy teams of George Burns and Gracie Allen, Bud Abbott and Lou Costello, Dean Martin and Jerry Lewis, and Lucille Ball and Desi Arnaz (also, Lucy and Vivian Vance, who played her sidekick, Ethel). Remember Stan Laurel and Oliver Hardy, or Jackie Gleason and Art Carney?

In every pairing, one of the members had a covert voice, while the other had an overt voice. Jackie Gleason, for example, was the overt voice—intense, outgoing, aggressive, while Art Carney, as Gleason's foil, was covert—indirect, less driven and less decisive, and rather plodding of sound.

President George Bush's voice is overt, but negative in his sound and style. Jesse Jackson is both overt and covert, depending upon time and place. Martin Luther King, Jr. was overt, and stunning in his warmth and charisma.

Oprah Winfrey is overt, as were the lately-paired team of Jane Pauley and Bryant Gumbel; no question also about Larry King, Peter Jennings, Dan Rather, and Tom Brokaw.

Dr. Ruth is covert, trying to be overt—and making it. Many show business people who have overt voices when performing may use covert voices off stage.

Many think overt voices, being the more dynamic, would command the most attention. That isn't always the case. A covert voice can be most appealing, showing subdued strength and sensitivity. The two voice types, in their own ways, can be used to a winning advantage.

THE MONEY SOUND—A WINNING VOICE

Some voices are so different and noticeable they become winning voices for the individuals using them. I am not recommending you imitate these voices; I am simply pointing out that these voices are not only conspicuous but also extremely profitable as a calling card and trademark. Some are well- used voices; some are not. But they are all money voices, that is they make money for the persons using them.

The list of top money voices is ever changing. Inevitably, the selection must be limited to people who are highly visible. Rather, they are audibly visible.

Here are thirteen of the best money voices in America. Each has a distinctive sound that is worth a fortune.

1. *Former President Reagan*—with his voice he could replace all television news anchors. Politics aside, he continues to have the most trusted voice in America. True grit, and more.

2. *Dr. Ruth Westheimer*—the most unforgettable voice of our time. Once you hear her, you are never the same again.

3. *Henry Kissinger*—sounds like his batteries are worn down. He makes Sylvester Stallone sound great.

4. *Joan Rivers*—a voice ahead of her times. When she talks, E.F. Hutton listens.

5. *Dennis Weaver*—makes you think the Old West is alive and well.

6. *Roseanne Barr*—who sounds but doesn't look like Mae West.

7. *Mr. Rogers*—caution: for kids only.

8. *Julia Child*—sounds like she's wearing tight clothing that is pinching.

9. *Sylvester Stallone*—the greatest mumbler of our day, replacing Marlon Brando.

10. *Woody Allen*—he has an aura of doubt, anxiety and insecurity. A nebbish to the core.

11. *Paul Harvey*—super-charged voice, ideal for morning wake-up calls.

12. *Telly Savalas*—everybody loves ya, baby.

13. *Michael Jackson*, the singer—who seldom speaks in public.

Rounding out the "top 30" are: Kirk Douglas, Bob Hope, Pee Wee Herman, Howard Cosell, David Brinkley, Clint Eastwood, Gregory Peck, Katherine Hepburn, Sandy Duncan, Tiny Tim, Roger Moore, Walter Cronkite, Don Adams, Suzanne Pleshette, Brenda Vaccaro, Bea Arthur, and James Stewart.

Arthur Godfrey, one of the greatest salesmen of all time, ranks high on the list of "Hall of Fame" money voices. So do Humphrey Bogart, Walter Brennan, Ronald Colman, Bert Lahr, Margaret Hamilton, Orson Welles, Charles Boyer, Jack Benny, Henry Fonda, Rosalind Russell, John Wayne, Peter Lorre, Rod Serling, Gary Cooper, Richard Burton, Sydney Greenstreet, Marilyn Monroe, and Cary Grant.

HOW TO BE HEARD, LISTENED TO, AND LIKED

There was a time, many years ago, when communication was either in person or by the written word. Today, people rely on voice more than ever before. It has been estimated that up to 89% of all communication is by voice.

Voices come flying at us from all directions, across dinner tables and desk tops, through loud speakers and intercoms, on radio and television. Communication has become an art, but the key to being heard, listened to, and liked is *sound*.

Some voices have a feel-good sound. They touch you; you trust them. They make you *want* to listen. Others make you cringe. You probably can name three or four of your favorite voices, and a like number of your least favorite.

It may surprise you to know that most of our top public speakers *learned* how to use their voices? That includes everyone from Dan Rather and Diane Sawyer to, yes, even former President Ronald Reagan.

They, like you, were born with the God-given ability to have good and great voices. But you need direction to make your true, natural voice speak for you. You have to learn whether you should talk higher or lower in pitch, how to focus your voice, and how to breathe correctly for speech.

Ronald Reagan learned to speak correctly long before he was elected to public office, and he never forgot those lessons. He has the most trusted voice in America. He is the best example of where a good voice can take you— and how it can help you stay there. His voice is his personality; he is perceived as a "nice guy." People relate to him because of his voice.

Reagan is without a doubt the greatest communicator of our time. Despite his years, his voice shows signs of aging only now and then. He may sound *tired* on occasion, but seldom old. Bob Hope, who is eight years Reagan's senior, has a voice that sounds as young and sprightly as ever, without a hint of voice trouble or fatigue. That is because he learned how to speak correctly, too.

No matter what your age, if you are using your voice correctly, there is no reason to lose your voice until you draw your last breath, barring a severe medical problem affecting the voice. In fact, there is no reason not to have a feel-good, sound-good voice that communicates who you are to the world. When you have a voice that talks for you, people pay attention.

VOICES IN THE CROWD (PARTY TALK)

It is almost inevitable that you won't come home from a cocktail party with a clear voice. It is also a good bet, depending upon how talkative you are, that your neck muscles will ache and you will have trouble speaking for the following few days.

Parties, sporting events, and other large gatherings are not only fun but great places to meet people and make deals. They are also rough on voices. That's because you talk, and keep on talking, despite the clatter of the surrounding crowd. You try to talk under the noise, over it, around it, above it—and nothing helps. You talk and you talk, and by the end of the evening, you have very little or nothing left. Your voice is either going or gone.

Most people never think about their voice when they are headed for a fun time. Even if they did, they would probably forget once the party got rolling and the refreshments started taking hold. So they talk on and on, pushing their voice, forcing it, squeezing it—losing it. By the time they feel something going wrong in their throat, it may be too late. The simplest way to deal with the problem is not to talk at all. That, of course, is impossible. The next best solution is to talk very little, which is not acceptable.

What can they, or you do? Try this:

If you are a man with a low-pitched voice, in the bass range, talk in the upper portion of that range or switch to a low baritone, but be sure to use the mask focus. If you are a low baritone, raise your pitch and speak in a little higher range. The same holds true for women with low contralto voices. Move to a slightly higher range and re-member, focus in the mask. The higher pitched voices are easier to hear and understand, easier to project, and less fatiguing on the throat and voice.

People who insist upon keeping the voice focused in the lower throat, and pitched low, are lost before they start. The noise level at public gatherings has been measured by physicists, and they tell us the din is too overpowering for the normal voice to hold its own. To be heard above crowd noise without getting a sore throat, it is wisest to speak in a higher pitch and with mask focus.

If you feel you cannot comfortably raise your pitch, or if you in-sist on speaking in your habitual voice because the change may harm your voice image, you have several other options. Stick close to your group and speak into the listeners' ears when you have something to say. Also, stay away from the center of noisy conversations. If you are able to maneuver people, try to relocate the conversation to the fringes of the party.

You don't have to strain your voice and throat when you talk in crowds. Raise your pitch, not your volume, talk in the mask, and talk *into* (not above or below) noise; you should feel better after the hoopla is over.

QUESTIONS & ANSWERS

Q: **Can "over-talking" tire the voice?**

A: If you are misusing or abusing your voice, it will probably tire and give out. But, if you are using your natural voice, you'll be able to talk as much as you want or need to talk under normal circumstances. "Over-talking" doesn't exist with a healthy, natural voice.

Q: Do many people have a monotone voice?

A: In my opinion, many people have poor voices, but not many have a true monotone voice: that is, a voice that has no variation of pitch, tone or volume. However, to the average listener, a voice that is boring, dull, lifeless, or makes little or no impression, often may be termed "monotone."

Q: My girlfriend wants me to listen to myself and find out about my voice. She says voices "type" a person. Is that true?

A: Yes, your voice is your identification. It reveals, often louder than words, if you are strong or wimpy, overt or covert, cheerful or whiny, sincere or not. The label you are given may not truly represent you or your personality, but that's the way it is. People often accept you—or reject you— by what your voice tells them, at least until they get to know you much better.

Chapter 6
The Colors of Voice

THE SOUNDS THAT REPRESENT US

The sound of your voice can affect you socially and professionally. An outgoing, strong, healthy voice is listened to and liked. A voice that is troubled, tense, distant and inaudible is a turn-off.

To hear Harry on the phone, or even in person, you would swear he is one of America's "most wanted." He sounds rough and tough, quite intimidating, but actually, he is a pussycat. Harry's friends overlook his voice, knowing it doesn't represent the real Harry. People who don't know him tend to shrink away. Harry is often offended by this reaction, but he won't be much longer. He has found his new voice—a higher-pitched, gentler voice—and he is practicing to retain it.

Another patient, Jan, used to speak in a sexy, sultry tone like Lauren Bacall. Lowering the voice to sound sensuous is quite common, but Jan talked "sexy" all the time, and it caused her problems. "I don't know why men come on so strong to me," she confided one day. "I'm not looking for anyone." Jan truly didn't realize the "vibes" she was sending out with her voice. She was unintentionally speaking in a "come hither" way.

Your voice can turn people off when you want to turn them on, and it can turn people on when you don't mean to. Everyone relates to sound. Such is the power of the voice.

You probably don't realize what you are doing with your voice, or how you are reaching out and touching people with its sound. When you first listen to yourself on tape, you may be surprised (if not shocked) at what you hear. You swear the voice on the playback is not you—or the you that you hear in your head. But it *is* you and though, like a lot of people, you don't like that other voice, you don't do anything about it. Instead of improving your voice, you go on sounding the way you always have.

Most successful people have voices that represent them as they really are. Others, whose voices are not fully effective, have learned to talk in a manner that commands respect and attention.

GAMES PEOPLE PLAY WITH THEIR VOICES

Actors may talk one way on stage, and another way in person. Doctors may have one voice for their patients and another voice at home. So may attorneys, executives, salespeople, teachers, and just about everyone who deals with the public. Nearly all "play games" with their voices. Chances are, so do you.

Have you ever noticed that you talk differently on the phone than you do when you are face to face with someone? Or that your phone voice differs from call to call? You talk one way with men and another way with women. You have a voice for friends and a voice for strangers and business associates. You have yet another voice for children and babies—a softer, gentler, more *natural* voice.

Your voice changes with the roles you assume throughout the day. In the office, you want to sound assured and assertive. At home, in a more relaxed atmosphere, you are less cautious about the way you speak.

Most people play the voice game without realizing it. Their voices change automatically, guided by mood, pressures, environment. Others play the game intentionally and so adroitly that their voices often become weapons. You've heard that voice, and may even have been a target at times. It is the voice that lashes out. It is often fierce, bombastic, and intimidating. People use that voice to make a point. The problem is, they often harm themselves physically in the process. They speak from the lower throat, pressing and straining, which not only irritates their throats but hurts their voices.

You can use different voices without pushing or hurting yourself, so long as you remember to keep the tone focus in the mask and use your natural pitch range. A different voice for different places or different people can be enjoyable, and can help make the impression you want to make.

VOICES FROM THE HEART (PET TALK)

As noted earlier, people use different voices for different situations. The voice people use to speak to pets is called "pet talk," and it truly comes from the heart.

Pet talk makes your voice warmer, more in *touch*. That is because pets humanize us. They break down our inhibitions and bring us back to ourselves, both in voice and in feelings. They allow us to behave more like we really are, if only for a little while.

"People talk"—that is, the way you talk to people—is often hard, formal, and stressful. Pet talk is endearing, easy, relaxed, and friendly.

When speaking with pets, or about pets (especially your own), another voice emerges. However, keep in mind that your pet talk voice simply reflects your ability to use different voices. It does not portray your natural voice. Imagine you have a pet with you now, and say a few words. Notice the ease in your voice, the spark, the friendliness. While the pet talk voice may not have the correct pitch or tone focus, it has a friendliness and gentleness that you may want to use in everyday conversation.

COLOR COORDINATING YOUR VOICE

When Bonnie called to set up an appointment, she didn't have to tell me what was wrong. Her voice was thin, light, airy. It was a voice without substance, one that people seldom take seriously. I tried to picture what she looked like based on her voice. A rather mousy young lady immediately came to mind.

Bonnie was young, but definitely not mousy. She was stunning to see, with a mind to match. But when she opened her mouth, the sound of her voice diminished her beauty and intelligence. "When I talk, people ignore me," Bonnie confessed. "My voice simply doesn't work for me."

Being attractive, bright, and articulate didn't help Bonnie when her voice downplayed who she really was.

"Is there hope for me?" she asked.

Not only was there hope, but she could have a voice to match her beauty, intelligence, ability, and potential. All she needed was direction. "Will you let me color coordinate your voice?" I asked.

Bonnie could not wait to get started.

She hummed, and I listened. "But I sound too loud," she said uneasily. She wasn't loud, but to her, changing from one voice to another, it seemed loud.

Bonnie's new voice was better, more effective and *different*. It was stronger, more confident, more believable, and colored with a new range of sounds and inflections. But she would have to become accustomed to it, grow to like it, until she could use it easily and naturally.

Finding and keeping your real, winning voice is like being on a diet. Unless you keep at it, it works only for a while, then you are right back where you started. If you work at reducing on an regular basis, however, your eating habits will change and, in time, the diet should show results.

The same is true for the voice.

Your new voice can represent you. It should become your trademark, your personal identification. You should not sound like anybody else. Your voice should present you at your best.

HOW TO LOSE OR SOFTEN YOUR ACCENT

Recently, an article in a major magazine reported on the rush of young urban professionals to shed their regional accents, twangs and drawls, which they feared might inhibit them socially or professionally. It is true that many people are concerned about their accents, but they are not all young. People of all ages believe that accents are stumbling blocks in their efforts to improve themselves.

Accents tend to call attention to the individual, rather than to what he or she is saying. There may be stigmas associated with accents, both domestic and foreign.

I love accents and I love New York. When I was growing up I spoke in a nasal New Yorkese, which I learned from my family and friends. Sounding like everyone else was fine as a youngster; it made me feel like I belonged. But as I got older I wanted to be more than just a sound-alike. I wanted people to notice me, the *real* me, and one of the first things I set out to improve was my voice.

As I mentioned, I love accents. They are money in the bank for some people, and an asset in many occupations. An English pub or French restaurant would lose charm and authenticity without accented waiters or waitresses. English accents add refinement and a touch of class to some establishments. Victor Borge would not be Victor Borge without his accent. How about Jackie Mason? Cyndi Lauper? Dr. Ruth? There have been hundreds of famous accents over the years. Many have been real, others exaggerated or put-on (games people play). Not all accents are endearing or attractive, however. Some work; too many others don't. Mine didn't work for me.

It was a struggle for me to lose my accent. I worked hard at it, and it took many months. That was before I discovered this simple secret: by changing the voice most accents are markedly diminished. In other words, you cannot easily retain an accent with a new voice. The key is a *new voice identity*.

The fastest, easiest way to soften an accent is to shift your voice to its natural pitch. When you change your pitch, you basically refocus your tone. The tone, believe it or not, is an essential item in creating and establishing an accent. With most people—not all—changing your voice greatly reduces the accent.

THE TELEPHONE VOICE

The host of a television talk show once asked me, "How can you tell if a voice is right or wrong just by hearing it on a phone, without seeing the person?"

I held my hand up to his face. "How many fingers?" I asked.

"Five," he answered.

"How do you know?"

"I can see them," he responded.

"Well," I said, "when it comes to voice, I can *hear* it. That's my job."

I wasn't being flip, only honest. I listen to voices every day, and the majority of them are problem voices that can be easily corrected. Many problem voices begin with the telephone.

One client, JoAnn, is a very astute businesswoman. She runs four companies, which necessitates a lot of phone talk. "I don't know why it happens," she said, "but as soon as I start talking on the phone, my voice begins to fail. It goes hoarse in a few minutes, and I find myself straining to talk. Before I know it, I am clearing my throat."

JoAnn told me that when she talks with friends her voice is clear and easy. But when she talks business she runs into trouble.

"Why do you think that is?" I asked.

JoAnn thought for a moment. "I'm not really conscious of it, but I know I talk differently when business is involved. I'm more on guard and reserved. I'm careful what I say. With friends I seem to talk more naturally."

Many people have JoAnn's problem. On important calls, especially at work, they use a different voice, a business voice. They try to keep the volume down, and, in the process, drop the pitch and the tone focus into the lower throat. This placement causes their throats to ache and their voices to lose power. They tire easily. The more they talk, the less they feel like talking.

In today's world, talking on the telephone is not only necessary but often the key to a successful career. Communicating by telephone need not be an ordeal. It can be fun and profitable if you use your voice correctly—by keeping it up in the mask area.

Remember, practice throughout the day, a second here, a second there. In public, say "um-hmm" (people love to have you agree with them, or at least show you are listening). In private, go back to the Cooper Instant Voice Press to confirm or reinforce your correct voice placement. And, hum your thoughts, and then say them aloud so you get used to the new natural voice.

WAKE UP YOUR MORNING VOICE

When you get up in the morning, your voice usually doesn't get up with you. It drags and groans. It sputters. You might refrain from talking until you have a cup of coffee or start moving around. Smart thing to do.

The morning voice can be either husky or clear. But it is often at the very bottom of the speaking range. That is because the body is essentially relaxed. There is nothing wrong with that unless you stay with that voice throughout the day. Some people do. Lots of men like the morning voice because it sounds masculine. Women often like it because it sounds sexy.

The morning voice really should not be your daily voice. It is something to lose as soon as you can, otherwise, you are talking trouble. The low-pitched morning voice can contribute to the onset and development of voice disorders.

If your morning voice is too low, it can be overcome easily by raising the pitch and tone focus as soon as you arise. If your normal voice is too high, this lower morning voice may be telling you your voice should be lower. Test it with the Cooper Instant Voice Press. After a while, it can become automatic to correct your pitch upon rising. You need only to remember to use "um-hmm" to clear your voice. Then hum "Happy Birthday" or try the Cooper Instant Voice Press. Focus your voice in the mask.

THE EXECUTIVE VOICE

Motion pictures are known for stereotyping men and women executives. Typical movie bosses are usually seen (and heard) as domineering, rather pompous, with a commanding voice. Off-screen, however, executives are seldom that way. They are simply real people with real responsibilities.

Today's executive is well-dressed, and needs a voice to match—confident, knowledgeable, alive in appearance and sound.

The executive voice attracts listeners, involving them rather than turning them off. It has range and flexibility. At times it is warm and friendly, often it is firm, and generally it is dynamic, with a touch of pizazz.

The well-trained executive voice can speak in short bursts or over long stretches without tiring. It is well modulated, steady, and deceptive, for it can mask the persona behind it. It radiates self-confidence. It has authority.

Not all executive voices embody these qualities, for not all executives know how to use their voices for maximum effect. Many need to be trained in voice. They need to learn to focus their voices in the mask area, and to breathe from their midsections for proper breath control and support.

Simply put, the executive voice should be for everyone who wants to be successful.

EVERYONE 'BOBBLES' BUT THEY DON'T CALL IT STUTTERING

A stutterer once told me, "If I could talk, I'd be a great success." Many others have confided similar hopes and dreams. They truly believe that the ability to talk easily will make all the difference in the world—their world.

I was never one to subscribe to that rather rosy point of view, until I ran into a gentleman who stuttered severely. When he first came to see me, he could barely make himself understood, but he did manage to say, with great effort, "If I could talk, I would make a fortune."

The man was a lawyer. But he seldom came into direct contact with the public, as most lawyers do. He worked in the back offices, out of sight and sound.

I helped him to talk smoothly again, and he made a fortune. Once he regained his speech, he moved out of the back room, where he not only faced the public but worked with the public.

Stutterers, like spastic dysphonics, are forever afraid of talking, fearing they won't talk well. When they try to communicate, they actually show a physiological difference from the normal individual.

If you compared the chemical and physiological makeup of an individual who stutters to that of an individual who has stage fright, I believe you would find a marked similarity. For stutterers (and spastic dysphonics) it is as if they have a perpetual case of stage fright; the pressured situation is on-going. The very thought of speaking creates stress, fear, and anxiety.

But, the stutterer lives with false images, long settled and terribly defeating. He seeks perfection of speech, an illusion that becomes the tyranny of the "I should," as in "I should speak perfectly." He tries to avoid the normal things we all do—like hemming and hawing, repeating a sound or word, mispronouncing a word, inserting vocal sighs, and using "uhs" and "ahs"—all known as "bobbles." He thinks of how he is going to talk before he talks. Worse, he thinks about the words and sounds not coming out right and it becomes a self-defeating, self-fulfilling prophecy.

The stutterer is making himself stutter. He forces his tongue against the roof of his mouth, or tightens his lips, so that the sound can come out easily. But, by doing that, he stops the free flow of the tongue and lips, and makes the mouth a battleground for keeping in the sounds and holding back speech.

Years ago, Jane Froman was a great singing star. She was one of the most beloved singers of her day, yet few of her fans ever heard her speak. That is because she couldn't speak without stuttering. Today, we have Mel Tillis.

Mel Tillis stutters when he talks but not when he sings. Why? My explanation is Tillis breathes when singing. Singing requires breath support, as does speaking correctly. It is natural for a stutterer to forget to breathe when talking. He holds his breath, trying to talk without any air—without any breath support.

As a singer, Tillis is familiar with his material. He knows the words and feels relaxed singing them. And he knows that people like what he does. He achieved success as a singer, but as a talker? That's another matter. It is my opinion that he goes tense talking, fearing the unrehearsed words and sounds, and so he blocks and begins stuttering.

It is interesting to note that stutterers can often talk in a room alone, or talk to a cat or a dog, without stuttering. The reason is, they have no fear of judgment from others or from themselves. They are more relaxed, making it easier for them to express themselves. The breathing is relaxed and normal. Distraction also helps. Distract the stutterer from his speech by shaking his hand and, presto, he can become a normal talker. Hand shaking, or any distraction, takes the mind off speech sounds and lets nature take its course. Talking should be spontaneous, and the stutterer isn't spontaneous when talking.

Non-stutterers also often have difficulty being spontaneous and their speech is seldom perfect. Have you noticed how few people can talk without inserting "uhs" and "ums" into their conversation? And how about the thought-provoking "you know"?

Of course, it's a rare answer that isn't prefaced by "Well ... "

Well-known author and speaker William F. Buckley repeats his words and hums on sounds (carrying over his hum from one word to another), making his speech a composite of "ohs," "ahs," hums and the other normal irregularities that constitute speech. I suggest that stutterers watch him as an example of how a normal person talks, and leave behind their dreams of perfect speech. Also, watch TV talk shows and listen to radio talk shows. Listen to how normal talkers constantly bobble when they talk. It is okay to bobble. Everybody bobbles. Stutterers try not to, and stutter.

Stutterers can talk and be successful. But they must get away from their ideas of perfection, which make speaking laborious and painful. Voice and speech not only should be but also can be easy and fun.

QUESTIONS & ANSWERS

Q: **My boss says I need to put some color in my voice. I've never heard the word "color" used to describe the voice. What does he really mean?**

A: Without shadings, the voice is colorless. Henry Kissinger's voice has no color. It is boring. It drones. So what your boss may really be telling you, in a polite way, is that your voice isn't doing its job.

Q: **I have a Midwestern accent. Some people think it is quaint and interesting, while others think it is funny that I don't do something about it. What do you think?**

A: Many people are self-conscious about their accents, especially if they are relocated to another state or country. An accent, however, can be a plus, particularly in business. It can give you a distinctive sound that gets you heard, listened to, liked, and even hired. The bottom line is, if the accent doesn't bother you, or get in your way, why do anything about it?

Q: **For years, I have apparently given offense by my "excited" voice. People have commented about it, and mentioned it to me in the spirit of frankness and friendliness, but I have never really understood their comments or views. That is until recently, when I actually listened to my own voice. It sounded petulant and carping. It had the tone of one given** to extreme surprise that some event had taken place or that someone had done something of note. **What can I do about my "excited" voice?**

A: An excited tone or sound is fine for appropriate occasions, when it is real and natural. But carried over to all conditions, circumstances and events, it bores and fatigues. Now that you are aware of your problem, you can take the first step in correcting it. A lower pitch should help you speak in a more deliberate and paced manner, with less staccato volume. Also, try slowing down your rate of speech.

Q: **How do you know if your voice is really representing you? I mean, showing your personality and your being?**

A: You don't. People dress a certain way because it represents them. On the other hand, people use a voice because they have always used it, not because it represents them. They don't know what voice they are using, or how to use it. They simply use a voice. By voice training and insight, you can develop your voice and find out if you are using your voice to your best advantage.

Q: **When I talk to children, why does my speaking voice go up in pitch? And, when speaking to their parents, why does it get lower?**

A: Children allow you to relax and let your guard down. Parents are people you have to confront or impress, and so you may use a lower "put on" voice, if the low-pitched voice is one that you feel implies authority and strengthens your image.

Q: **Do all people hear my voice the same way?**

A: Your voice is heard the same way, but people don't react to it the same way. The sound of your voice is influenced by an individual's voice images, so the tone you use is received as either appealing or unappealing. People like or dislike it according to their own voice tastes and experiences.

Q: **My new job requires me to get up earlier than usual. With my new, earlier hours, I have noticed that my voice is very**

low when I begin to talk in the morning. People tell me they like the low voice, and I appreciate the praise. I like the low voice too, but the more I use it in the morning, the less I can talk through the day. Is there some connection between my low morning voice and my lack of voice later in the day?

A: Definitely. The morning voice is, for a number of people, a very low voice. You need to raise your morning voice; try speaking with the voice you had before you began your new job. The low morning voice is not to be used extensively in talking. It is simply the most relaxed voice in your speaking range, the bottom of your voice range, and it is tiring to use too long. It fatigues your throat muscles, and tires your voice. A number of voice problems arise because people use the low morning voice. They never connect the voice problem as you did. Congratulations.

Chapter 7

Tense and Stressful Voices

HOW TO CONTROL YOUR VOICE UNDER STRESS

We've all heard about "big games." They come along every year in every sport, and at all levels of play: high school, college, and professional. Coaches spend long hours preparing themselves and their players so that their teams will be at their peak physically, mentally and emotionally. Motivational pep talks are part of the preparation, yet care must be taken not to go overboard.

When teams start off poorly, even the best conceived game plan can be thrown out of kilter. Sportscasters often mention, especially after early missed baskets or poorly thrown passes, that a player (if not the entire team) looks out of sync, is lacking poise and control, or is simply too charged up. A knowing "Once they settle down. . ." generally follows. What it all boils down to is the jitters—tension and stress.

A team playing out of control self-destructs. It is that way with your voice, too. Your voice should sound like a finely tuned machine. Smooth, steady, strong. But use it incorrectly over a long period of time, like driving a car in the wrong gear, and it will fail.

Tension and stress due to overwork, family or money troubles, can do more than create or contribute to a voice problem. If not controlled, the problem can steadily worsen, particularly if other factors such as smoking, drinking and illness are involved. The good news is that you need not have a stress-related voice problem. You can even rescue your voice if you are in a stressful situation. Some people are simply unable to eliminate stress from their lives.

The key factor is to learn how to control your natural voice. Some people do it instinctively; others must learn.

Most people let stress go to their lower throats, and it shows in their voices through a squeezed, tired, troubled sound. Such a voice can strain your career and personal relationships. Physically, it can damage your throat and result in nodes, polyps, contact ulcers, and worse. It can also lead to a strangled voice—one that sounds like someone is throttling you as you talk.

Of course, it isn't easy to go about speaking in a relaxed way when, in reality, you are not. The secret is to be aware of your focused voice; let the sound produced from the vocal cords reach out and touch your lips and nose, and resonate there. A properly used voice should relax you, knowing that you sound strong, dynamic, confident. There is no need to relax the entire body to sound good; but knowing that you sound good should help you relax.

You can relax your voice by humming. If you are among other people, a near-silent hum or a hummed response ("um-hmm") should help you place your voice correctly. With practice, you should soon have the feel of it.

MAKING STRESS WORK FOR YOU THROUGH YOUR VOICE

We all use adrenaline, our body's natural stimulant, to push us in our drive to be a winner. It gives us a competitive rush. But there is a downside to all that energy, especially in professional life. It used to be called "nerves." Today, it is *stress*.

Stress makes your body tense, and puts you on edge. Your voice responds by going too high or too low in pitch, often hugging the sensitive lower throat. It becomes rough and gravelly; words crack in mid-sentence. Clearing your throat doesn't help. You appear awkward and tentative. Your sound is not one of confidence.

People who are in stressful situations tend to hold their breath. It can happen at any time, no matter where you are, while driving, during an office meeting or a family dinner. Under stress your body stiffens and breathing becomes irregular, even stops for a time.

A patient with a high-pressure job recently visited my office. Speaking on the phone makes him tense, he told me. He is on the phone a lot at work, and his voice gives out. I asked him to count from one to ten. When he did, he held his breath.

"Why did you do that?" I asked.

"I don't know," he responded.

"Is that how you talk on the phone at work?"

"I guess so," he replied. "I hadn't thought about it."

I told him to have his secretary either take his calls or hold them until later in the day when he felt he could concentrate on his voice. He looked at me as if I were joking. When he discovered I wasn't, he tried my suggestion. And it worked. It worked so well, in fact, that he is now able to talk through his tension rather than suppress it.

It may work for you too. But not everyone has a secretary to run interference, or the luxury of being able to hold calls until another time. The important point, however, is to remember to use your natural voice. To do that, you must breathe regularly and from the midsection.

Once you learn to use your voice correctly, stress can actually work *for* you, instead of against you. It doesn't matter who you are or what you do, that extra throb generated by nerves can turn a so-so voice into a winner, making it even easier to listen to—and persuasive.

Actors are probably the best example. It is a rare actor who doesn't have "butterflies" before a performance, yet they are able to step on stage, before a camera or microphone, with voices that are extra alive, rich and full. There is no better spokesman than former President Reagan. As an actor, he learned how to use his voice. As President, that voice charmed countless millions. No matter how he felt personally, he sounded relaxed, warm, and completely confident.

The lesson, then, is: Do not try to hide your nerves, use them. Let your voice speak out, not down. Speak up, but not high. Keep your voice even, and in the middle of your range. And breathe evenly. Now, you can relax, your voice is really speaking for you.

THE JOB INTERVIEW—WHAT YOUR VOICE SAYS ABOUT YOU

Years ago, when I first started doing live radio interviews, a good friend (who also happens to be a top publicist) offered some advice. He told me: "The first 10 to 20 seconds make all the difference in the world for connecting or not connecting with your audience. Your voice will get you tuned in or tuned out." Not long after that, the book editor at a major publishing house imparted some helpful inside information. He said, "If a manuscript doesn't excite me in the first twenty pages, it is out the door."

What these two executives, both leaders in their fields, were saying was: Unless you make an immediate positive impression, forget it.

Nowhere do these words hit home more than in a job interview. You may dress beautifully, have an impressive resume, and ooze with confidence. But the minute you open your mouth, the illusion may be shattered.

My publicist friend, who works closely with a number of prominent companies, has told me repeatedly about the importance of voice in a job interview. The voice tells all, he says, and many people are simply passed over because of their voices.

Indeed, the voice *does* tell all. It tells if you are tense, troubled, angry, distant, formal, or indifferent. It tells if you are aggressive, brash, confident, insecure, strong or weak. The view from the outside may be terrific, but your voice gives the inner you away. And the person on the other side of the desk may not like what he or she hears.

All too often, the voice makes the difference between getting hired and walking away empty handed. Few people truly realize, however, that their voices are selling them short. Most people don't want to offend, so nothing is said. It is simply "Hello" and "Thanks for coming in." And you are left to believe that you are not fully qualified (not necessarily true) or that you did not make a good impression (absolutely true).

What do *you* think your voice says about you? Do you feel it has a confident, strong, healthy sound? Or is it weak and wimpy, the type of voice even *you* feel uncomfortable being around?

There is no better time than now to find out. Say a few sentences into your tape recorder and then listen to the playback. No matter what you hear, there is almost always room for improvement. Hum the first line of "Happy Birthday" or "Row, Row, Row Your Boat," the most basic exercise, to get you started. Then say it aloud—don't sing it—as you hummed it. Follow with the "um-hmm" exercises. Feel the "buzz" that indicates your voice is placed correctly in the mask area? You should feel a tingle, a slight ring, about your lips and nose. Feel it?

Record your voice once again. Can you hear the difference between the two recordings? That is what others hear.

YOUR VOICE IS YOUR FORTUNE

You've seen how people respond to a person's voice. You know how you respond. Words are one thing, but voice is something else.

Your voice can make people like you or dislike you. It can get you hired or fired. A strong, healthy voice opens doors and creates opportunities . Your voice is a wondrous, personal identification card. And it can be your fortune if you use it correctly, naturally.

A voice that is used properly triggers a positive response. It can make friends with people next to you, across the room or miles away—in person or on the phone. No matter what level of success you have reached, you can achieve more with a voice that commands respect and attention.

You are not stuck with a voice you don't like or one that is used improperly. If you feel you have a poor, troubled voice (your tape recorder will tell you when even your best friends won't!) then make it richer, stronger, fuller. You can, by practicing the simple exercises for only minutes a day, until your winning voice becomes habitual. How long that will take is up to you .

Once again, to locate your winning voice, hum the first bar of "Happy Birthday" or "Row, Row, Row Your Boat." Remember, it is important to feel the slight balanced vibration around your nose and mouth as you hum.

Another good exercise is "um-hmm" (say it casually as if responding to a friend in conversation, with your lips closed).

Repeat these exercises from time to time each day and you should be on your way.

QUESTIONS & ANSWERS

Q: Do nerves cause a voice problem?

A: Nerves make your body tense, and you, edgy. Your voice responds by going too high, or too low in pitch, often hugging the lower throat. You may think that by talking lower you sound controlled, and that no one will know you are nervous or tense. The opposite is really true. Talking in the lower throat is a dead giveaway. But nerves can be handled in a positive way by making them work *for* you, not against you.

Nerves create the extra throb that stimulates drive and ambitions. Creative people use nerves, when unable to come up with answers, to write out or talk out their tensions. Actors use nerves to give their voices that winning performance. Jack, an executive in your company, confides that he is tight as a bowstring. "But you don't sound it," you tell him. Jack may not believe you, but it's true. He doesn't show stress or tension through his voice. It shows up in other places. Chances are he has stomach problems or migraine headaches.

Don't try to hide your nerves. Use them to your advantage. Speak out, not down. Speak up, but not high. Keep it even and in the middle of your range. But don't let your voice be controlled by your nerves. If you ask anyone doing anything that takes effort, patience and skill, they will probably tell you they experience nerves now and then, if not often. They simply make their nerves work for them.

Q: Does a tense personality cause voice trouble?

A: Many people with voice troubles are tense, but their voice troubles are not caused by tension. They simply don't know how to use their voices. When the voice is used correctly, it sounds open, feels better, and people respond in a more positive way.

Q: What can a better voice do for you?

A: When you talk, people listen. For a little while, anyway. Your voice can turn people on or off. The sad part is, most voices don't do anything for people. They may be heard, but they probably aren't liked, listened to, or wanted.

Q: **Is it true that a shot of brandy helps smooth out the voice and tone?**

A: Brandy relaxes the body, and often the mind. A small amount of brandy is relaxing, but too much brandy and you have little voice control, and less voice.

Q: **My voice is hoarse almost all the time. My doctor says there is nothing medically wrong, only that I am using my voice incorrectly. How is that? I have been using this voice for 45 years. Why should it get hoarse now?**

A: Your doctor is right. Your voice is hoarse because you are misusing it. It happens at different ages because of different capacities to withstand vocal misuse. You must learn to use your voice properly or it will probably remain hoarse and deteriorate further, possibly causing a medical problem.

Q: **How do you make a tense person less tense through the right voice?**

A: People everywhere are under stress, simply because stress and tension are common in today's society. But you needn't show tension, or express it through your voice. Tension often causes the voice to rise in pitch. You can mask tension by talking in your natural range, with mask focus, rather than in the lower throat or pitching your voice too high. This makes your voice sound easy and open and friendly which makes others more relaxed with you and, in turn, you at ease with them. In addition, physical exercise can help reduce stress and tension and thereby help relax the speaking voice.

Chapter 8

How to Talk in Public and Like It . . . as Easy as 1-2-3

A BEGINNER'S INTRODUCTION TO TALKING IN PUBLIC OR PUBLIC SPEAKING

This chapter offers a natural approach to talking in public, making it as easy as one-two-three. This approach is far different from anything you may have read or heard about before. It is for beginners who want to talk in public and be at ease, but don't know how and are overwhelmed by the prospect of public speaking.

First of all, I find the term public speaking inaccurate, a turn-off and frightening to most people; it creates a wrong image of what you have to do to talk in public. Giving a speech for the beginning public speaker turns you into a robot, transforming you into someone other than you. It doesn't make you comfortable with yourself, or natural with the audience.

You can talk in private and you do. "You do have the gift of conversation," I tell my clients, "Use it. Don't give speeches." For the most part, speechifying is for the experienced, the professionals,

85

those polished and with long experience in dramatizing their views and themselves at the specific time and place. It is not for the beginning speaker who lacks training in public speaking, who doesn't have the means and training to keep in mind what he/she wants to say and the emotional ability to say it, combining the logos, the pathos, and the ethos of what makes for a good speech. A talk allows you to make your points and give information, and help you learn to compose yourself in public. So, give talks. Remember, talking in public is like chatting in private conversation. I want you to use the same style of talking in public that you use talking in private. The only difference is that when talking in public you need to know what you are talking about, and have the points you want to make organized. Be as engaging as you are when talking with friends, trying to get them to understand your point of view, your position, your feelings, or your thoughts. Talking in public often is but a few minutes experience—five or six, maybe ten or fifteen.

Modern public speaking is easy to understand if you think of it as **one person talking in an organized manner to one audience in the same conversational style in which people talk in private. This is the secret to talking in public and liking it.**

Also, keep in mind all that you have learned about natural voice production. Keep your voice focused and breathe correctly, just as you do when you are talking in private.

Before you begin, however, there are a few things you need to know about talking in public or, as it is most commonly called, public speaking. Let's start by looking at what public speaking is—and what it is not.

What is Talking in Public or Public Speaking? When you speak in public, you will be talking with an audience. It might be a small audience, or a large one that fills a room.

The smallest possible audience consists of one person who listens while the speaker is talking. An example of this is the TV talk show host who interviews a guest. While the host is talking, his/her guest is the audience. But while the guest is talking, the host does the listening. The TV viewers actually comprise a much larger audience, numbering thousands or even millions. But the actual in-person program involves only two people.

This same TV show host might appear in public, personally addressing an audience of several hundred people. In such a case, he/she would talk with the audience in much the same way he/she would talk with one guest—by treating the audience as if it were one collective person.

What Talking in Public or Public Speaking Is Not. Today's public speaking no longer involves a formalized technique that comes out of a textbook. Learning the formal approach to public speaking by reading textbooks may be necessary for students who need to know the history of public speaking; but the average person who talks in public does not need theory as outlined in books. No one can learn to be a public speaker by reading about it. You need experience, and the only way to get that experience is to stand up and start talking in public.

Two Approaches To Public Speaking. Centuries ago in ancient Greece, there were two schools of thought about public speaking. Both approaches stressed formal oratorical speaking. "Speechifying," or the oratorical style, is no longer in vogue for general public speakers.

Aristotle believed the way to learn public speaking was to learn the theory, then put it into practice. He practiced what he taught. Isocrates, however, disagreed with Aristotle. He advised that you speak, make mistakes, learn from mistakes, and then study the theory of what you did right and where you went wrong. But he studied *after* he gained experience.

Today's popular approach to public speaking embraces both of these methods. Some people learn theory before they begin giving speeches by employing the Aristotelian approach. Most people, however, especially newcomers to the field, tend to follow in the footsteps of Isocrates. They give public speaking a try, and then, if they are so inclined, they begin perfecting their techniques and learning theory so that talking in public becomes easier and more polished with each talk given.

Is Once Enough? Beginners who suffer stage fright often think they will never get into such a situation again. For them, it seems one public talk in a lifetime is enough.

After their initial nervousness passes, they may find they actually like talking in public. Once they are over being terrified, they get a taste of glory, and they can come to love public speaking. They want to know more about public speaking because, for them, once is not enough.

If you are one of these people, and chances are you will be, you will want to know more about public speaking as it applies to you.

Three Guidelines to Remember. There are three guidelines you should remember to be effective talking in public:

Practice public talking. Get up often, on different occasions, everywhere, and talk, talk,talk. I do. Before I talk publicly about a subject, anything in my field, I talk privately about it constantly. When the time comes for me to step before an audience, I am ready because I have talked endlessly on the topic. And people say I sound very natural.

Being natural takes practice. Practice getting on and off stage without making a federal case out of it. Get your experience, because practice is the key to getting you heard, listened to, and liked. In public speaking, practice is the only way to gain experience. Practice makes perfect. Practice makes permanent. But wrong practice makes permanently wrong, so practice correctly.

Be sincere. Be yourself. Speak from your heart about a subject you know well and like to talk about. To gain your practice, talk about something in which you have expertise. It can be any subject about which you are well informed, such as a hobby, art or craft. Or, perhaps, a technique you have developed for solving problems. You may have a true personal experience you think would interest others.

Be natural. Don't try to project an image that will impress the audience. It isn't necessary. If you are talking sincerely about something you know backward and forward, inside and out, you will be presenting the best image if you present your natural self.

As in day-to-day conversational speaking, the key to being liked and listened to rests in your being yourself. Tell what you know—simply, directly and openly—with perspective. Don't dawdle. Finish and leave the stage.

WHEN ALL EARS ARE ON YOU

You are standing alone in a spotlight at center stage, alone, before a hushed audience waiting for your first words. From the moment you were asked to speak before the group, you have been filled with fear. It started with an initial rush of anxiety and continued to build.

If this brief description sounds familiar, you are not alone. Recent surveys of a wide variety of professionals—executives, politicians, and entertainers—showed eighty-five percent fear public speaking more than anything, including snakes, disease, financial disaster, even death—which indicates that very few of us are immune to stage fright.

Despite America's fear of public speaking, more people are speaking before audiences than ever before. For some, it is a function of their executive positions; for others, it is necessary for advancement. The majority of these people have had little or no prior experience in public speaking.

Experienced or not, few people escape being nervous when in the spotlight. Everyone is concerned with what others think and feel about them. Talking in public, whether before friends or strangers, makes you aware of how vulnerable you are to a larger audience's thoughts and feelings.

STAGE FRIGHT

Maybe you won't experience stage fright.

You might be so naturally gifted at talking in public that you will never feel as if you are about to stop breathing once you are standing on the stage.

Maybe your knees won't begin shaking, or your stomach won't be fluttering with "butterflies." And maybe, just maybe, you won't become so self-conscious that your mind goes blank and your voice turns hoarse.

But if any or all of these symptoms should suddenly make you painfully aware you are facing a roomful of people, and you are so nervous it seems you can't continue, you will be experiencing stage fright.

A Natural Transition. Stage fright, the public speakers' "bug," is like the "flu." It passes.

How does a speaker shake stage fright? By talking in public. Again, and again, and again. It is like any skill, the more you have practiced, the easier it becomes.

There is a positive aspect to stage fright. It may seem like it is never going to end, but you do get over it. And you rid yourself of it by making yourself talk. You actually talk the stage fright away.

Stage fright is a natural transition from being the relaxed, private person you usually are to being a person who is now in the public spotlight. Its symptoms usually appear at the beginning of a talk because that is when the transition takes place.

Understanding the Cause. Stage fright is an effect. To treat the effect, you must understand the cause.

People who suffer stage fright are afraid of being judged by their audiences–*negatively* judged, to be precise. And that is unpleasant enough to frighten anyone.

So when a speaker suddenly sees rows of faces that appear to be staring at him, he tightens up in response. People really aren't staring. They are facing the speaker, waiting for him or her to tell them something they want to hear and they want to learn. The speaker is simply reacting to the deep-seated fear of being judged. Understanding what stage fright is can help you combat it if it should strike you.

When Stage Fright Hits. Stage fright hits many people before they set foot on stage. They might be so frightened of "making a speech" that they begin getting tense and nervous long before the actual date they are to appear.

They get so nervous they can make themselves sick. This gives them a good excuse for getting out of their speaking engagement, but it doesn't do much to help them overcome their fear of public speaking.

Others are more stalwart. Even knowing they might be hit with a case of stage fright, they muster their courage and go on with the speech anyway. These people usually find it is not as bad as they imagined. And each succeeding case of stage fright becomes milder as they gain more and more public speaking experience.

Changing Your Attitude. A change of attitude can chase away stage fright. Instead of reacting negatively to the audience, tell yourself that if the audience wasn't looking at you, you would be insulted. After all, your audience is focused on you because the people came to hear you talk. So they are looking at you out of respect and interest, not to be critical or judgmental. What could be more friendly than that?

If you suddenly become painfully aware that everyone is staring at you and you feel terrified (or as if you are about to freeze) change your attitude toward the audience. This is easy to accomplish if you will consider the audience to be a friend, one single friend comprised of many people, and think of yourself as talking with the audience, not as giving a speech.

FACTOR X

One of the most important factors in overcoming your fear is what I call "factor X." In simple terms, "factor X" is your personality, or rather, what happens to your personality when you step before an audience. Does it change or are you the same as in private?

Many people transform when on stage. Their personalities change dramatically. For instance, someone who is normally strong and confident may become just the opposite. Facing a crowd can do that. And that is where "factor X" comes in.

To be the best public talker you can be, be yourself. Don't try to be forceful if you are not. Don't try to be animated or humorous or anything you are not. Be yourself. Don't put on airs. Speak as you normally do, using words you normally use. If you assume another personality, one that is not yours, you detract from your presentation. You won't be successful that way. Remain conversationally informal as you do with friends, associates, acquaintances.

So how can you "be yourself" when you probably have never felt less like yourself? One way is to let your emotions come forth. If stage fright temporarily floods you with fear, don't stiffen up and hide what you are feeling. You'll get through it. Your audience will be pulling for you; they will understand. A lot of them have had stage fright too.

OVERCOMING INSECURITY

Most people who talk in public, for organizations and other assorted groups, are experts in their field. They know what to say; they simply fear saying it in public. They are terrified of taking their place at the podium, of being seen and heard, but any other times they are calm and collected. The reaction is normal, especially for anyone unaccustomed to talking before audiences.

Why the change?

An overwhelming fear brought on by insecurity. "What will people think of me?" they ask themselves. "What will they say of me? How will I come across? Can I get through it? What happens if ...?"

But when you talk in private conversation, do you ask yourself those questions? Of course you don't. In private conversation you talk spontaneously. At times, you may edit your thoughts before speaking, but you don't run scared. In public, you are scared because you are playing a role—the expert, the authority, the executive. You have something to say and you want to be sure you say it correctly. You can if you know your subject.

Knowing your subject thoroughly builds confidence, so it is important to do all your homework in advance. When you are familiar with your subject you can speak from a position of strength in an informal, more off-the-cuff manner which is more easily understood. That is essential, especially today. Years ago, speaking in public meant giving a regimented or formal speech. Now, good public speaking is less formal, if not informal. Audiences will no longer sit through long-winded oratories. Television has accustomed us to gathering information at a faster pace and presenting it in a less stilted manner.

A major concern of every public speaker is "What happens if ...?" The worst that can happen is you forget what you've planned to say. When words fail you, don't panic. You may stand momentarily with a blank expression and an open mouth, but all is not lost. Take a breath, move about a bit, pause and recapture your train of thought. Then start over. Do not try to recall or seek the exact word, phrase, or thought when it does not come readily to mind. Talk around the word or idea. Nobody is aware that you do not have the specifics in mind. Keep the flow of conversation going. Don't stand as if at loose ends saying "oh" and "ah," creating your own discomfort and making the audience uncomfortable. It will help if you outline the major points you want to cover on 3"x5" note cards. Then, if words fail, your notes can guide you along.

If Stage Fright Persists. It takes practice to overcome stage fright; but no matter how gifted you are as a public speaker, there will be times when it unexpectedly hits you.

Stage fright is the most shattering of all public speaking experiences. If it can happen to the most seasoned professionals (even the great veteran actress, Helen Hayes, and others admit to becoming ill with fear before stepping on stage to face a live audience), it can happen to you. It is best to prepare yourself for the inevitable.

If you have changed your attitude toward the audience and you still aren't able to capture the friendly, relaxed conversational atmosphere you had hoped to achieve between yourself and your listeners, take heart. There are techniques—tricks, actually—to get you through stage fright without anyone ever knowing.

Practice any of these tricks, which the most seasoned professional public speakers use when they are caught on stage with a case of jitters.

> **Move.** Move about freely on the stage, but not excessively. Too much movement is distracting, but some movement is natural. Lean on the podium or step out from behind it. Don't stand stiffly in one spot unless you are comfortable and at ease. Stage fright might make you feel as if you were numb all over, but you can loosen up by moving. Use gestures as you do in conversation; let your whole body get involved in your talk. Movement may help you talk in a more relaxed way, the way you normally talk in conversation. You might want to put one or both hands in your pocket(s). Do whatever is natural and within reason.

> **Focus on Someone.** Focus your attention on one person in the audience and briefly talk with him or her. Then choose another person in the audience. State a point, then turn to still someone else. Do it easily and smoothly, just as you do in conversation. Let your eyes and conversation wander sensibly. Involve the audience as you do friends and others in your conversation.

> If you find that stage fright prevents you from choosing one or two friendly faces to look into as you begin your talk, look at the whole audience in general and say to yourself, "That's my old friend, Bernie (or whoever). He's sure a friendly guy." Then talk to the group the way you would talk to Bernie, or Sheila, or John, or Mary, or the person you would like to imagine your audience to be. It

is important to look at them and not at the ceiling or into space. By focusing your attention on others, and becoming involved outside yourself, your self awareness and your stage fright—and its symptoms—should pass.

Talk Up. If your voice starts shaking, or if it begins sounding like a whisper, speak louder. Keep your voice focused in the mask, the area around the lips and nose. This will help your voice be energized and audible; it will have carrying power. The reason one's voice shakes during stage fright may be that the speaker himself/herself is shaking. By keeping the tone focused properly, you can help overcome voice shakiness and, with it, trembling of the body. (Note: see Chapter 7.)

Breathe. Inner shaking can make you feel as if you are losing your breath. If this happens, don't try to deliver long sentences in one breath. Breathe every three, four, or five seconds. Say a few words, then take a breath and continue talking. This, too, should help you overcome stage fright.

Continue to take a breath every three to five seconds and as needed throughout your speech. It is the natural way to breathe when talking, whether on or off the public speaker's platform. Tension, fear, and anxiety may cause you to hold your breath. You can't talk without air. Be sure to use midsection breath support.

Find Your Best Attitude. Every public talker who has survived stage fright has found the attitude best suited to his/her own public speaking needs. They have developed these attitudes by gaining experience as public talkers, by standing on their feet time and time again and talking, talking, talking. They talk until, at last, they are able to talk as comfortably to a group as they can talk in a private conversation with friends.

You must find your own best attitude, one that gives you

a feeling of control and ease, but not one of superiority. Speakers projecting attitudes of superiority come across as aggressive, negative and condescending. They talk down to their audiences, rather than talking with their listeners.

An audience would much prefer to hear a sincere speaker who may be struggling to overcome a case of stage fright to one who appears so perfect he/she is a notch or two above them.

Be sincere in your attitude toward your listeners. Talk *with* them, not over or around them.

MAKING PRIVATE CONVERSATION IN PUBLIC

When talking in public, always keep in mind that it should be the same as talking to a group of people you already know—friends, acquaintances, co-workers, or whomever. You are simply talking to a larger group than usual. It may be only slightly larger or it may be considerably more than you are used to facing, but you should talk to the audience as you do your friends. Remember, talking in public is merely a private chat made public. An exchange. Don't make it a big deal, and don't make it formal. Don't think in terms of "giving a speech." Think rather in terms of chatting with your audience. It can make all the difference in the world emotionally and psychologically to you. Chatting relaxes; giving a speech doesn't.

The more you talk in public, the more relaxed and confident you should become. To be the very best you can be, practice is essential. There is no substitute for it. You can't learn to play a piano by reading a book.

Practice talking at every opportunity. Volunteer to speak before groups of all sizes to help diminish your fears. When speaking in public, we tend to view the audience as the enemy. They aren't. These people have come to hear you.

The emphasis on casual, conversational public talking has made speaking easier than ever before. If you are wondering what approach to take, turn on your television or radio and listen. Johnny Carson, Oprah Winfrey, Phil Donahue, Sally Jessy Raphael, Arsenio Hall, Geraldo, David Letterman, and others are masters of the conversational approach.

Once again, it is essential to be fully familiar with your subject. Talk only on subjects you know. Don't bother with topics that stray from your area of expertise.

And remember, don't try to project an unnatural image when you step to the podium. You are the person the audience wants to hear, not someone else. Be yourself.

AMERICA'S SOFT SPOT

Most talking in public is simply giving information. Don't try to be witty if you aren't. Don't be overly dramatic or serious. Serious is boring, and the cardinal sin of public talking, or talking anywhere, is to bore the listener. Tell what you know in a simple, direct, open way, with perspective, and then stop.

Unless you are a good actor, don't act a part when you talk in public. Remember, be yourself. Talk naturally, as you normally would in private conversation. And don't hide behind titles. You may be someone with a long list of accomplishments, but an artificial attitude won't help your presentation. Be natural.

That isn't always easy, of course. Susan, a patient, was losing her voice when she came to me. To make matters worse, she had been asked to speak at a large meeting of company officials and employees. Susan was petrified. She was normally nervous anyway and it showed in her voice, which reacted to stress by gradually failing until she was unable to speak at all.

I tried to calm Susan by telling her to warm up before the meeting. "Practice your talk until it becomes automatic," I told her. "The president warms up. Comedians warm up. They don't go on cold; they rehearse and rehearse."

"But my bosses are tough," Susan countered. "They expect perfection."

"You don't have to be perfect to do a good job. Just know your material. Talk about it with people throughout the day. Weave portions of what you want to say into your conversations as you can. By doing so, you familiarize yourself with the material. Then give your views or position talking naturally and directly in a conversational manner. The people will love you."

The point is, when you talk about what you know, you talk from a position of strength. Many people speak from a position of weakness. They aren't sure of their subject, so they aren't sure of themselves. Talk from your area of strength, about what you know, and you can talk in a winning way.

CHOOSING THE RIGHT SUBJECT

Back in the early 1950's, people didn't talk as openly as they do today, particularly about their own experiences, and especially not in public. Public speaking was far more formal, and public speakers were much more reserved than they are today.

The trend that led to today's public speaking revolution began growing nationwide during the 1960's when the public started talking in vast numbers over the radio and television networks of America. They had things to say and, for the first time in American history, they had freedom of public speech in which to say them.

It was, and is, interesting, fascinating, revolutionary. People talked about everything from their personal sightings of unidentified flying objects to homespun methods for curing warts and natural remedies purported to cure cancer. Future overpopulation, birth control, gay rights, survival in the Nazi concentration camps, adjusting to deafness, overcoming frigidity, coping with computers, drugs, teen-age sex, and immigrants were all openly talked about. For the first time ever, people even discussed their own surgical sex changes before a listening public numbering in the millions. The "here's my true experience" movement continued to grow, through the 1970's and into the 1980's, spreading into the community-at-large.

Today, more people are talking in public than ever before in our country. But they are no longer doing it only over TV or radio. They are talking in schools, auditoriums, churches, banquet halls, meeting rooms, restaurants, and museums. They are speaking from platforms in parks, on campuses, and even on street corners. They are speaking from the community rooms of local Senior Citizen Centers, as well as Savings and Loan Associations. And they are speaking in seminars, workshops and specialized non-academic classes taught by people who may not hold university degrees, but who are experts in the subjects they are teaching.

Popular Personal Approach. When I discovered that listeners, including my professors in college, responded favorably when I was *being myself*, talking about a subject I knew and liked, using the same conversational style two friends would use when talking in private, I wasn't aware I was in on the beginning of a trend. All I knew was the personal approach to talking in public worked so well for me that I have been using it ever since. And I have encouraged my patients and clients to also practice the popular personal approach to talking in public.

What to Talk About. The first thing you should be concerned with is choosing your subject. You will enjoy giving your talk, and your audience will enjoy hearing it, if you talk about something you know about and are eager to discuss.

Is there a subject you feel so strongly about that the "will to fight" is aroused in you? If so, talk about it, provided it is suited to the audience you will be addressing. In other words, your talk should be well-suited to the occasion at which you will be speaking, and also should fit the time framework allotted for presenting your talk.

Life Experiences. The majority of public talks today fall into the life experience category. Speakers talk about things they learned in school; about things they have learned from life; about something they have learned from other people; about something they have learned themselves, and they talk about their field of expertise.

Each person is an expert at something, one thing that may have arisen out of a hobby, an illness or an unexpected situation that required an innovative personal solution. A person's field of expertise might have no actual bearing on his occupation or on the subject he majored in at school. Yes, you too, are an expert, perhaps at several things you have mastered through your own personal life experiences.

Many times a person gains expertise in something he/she has faced as a challenge—and has managed to surmount or solve.

The How-To-Do-It Talk. A popular approach to public speaking today is the "how-to-do-it" talk. The speaker introduces his/her subject, then tells the story of how he/she became an expert, and offers advice about how the audience can also benefit. He/she is talking about his/her own life experiences and how they might benefit the lives of his/her listeners.

You could be an expert at something as simple as making old fashioned chicken soup with real homemade noodles. Maybe you have an expert way to make a major cross-country move while coping with little children. Possibly you are a young widowed father left with five little children to raise. You might even know a unique way of traveling on a shoestring budget to places unfamiliar to most tourists. If this is the kind of talk you will be giving, remember that the audience is interested in what you have to say because they may benefit by your experience. Just be sure to talk about whatever you know well, do best and like most.

The "How It Happened To Me" Talk. This type of talk relates a true story, one that usually changed the speaker's life. The word *I* is frequently used, since it is a true experience. Such a talk sometimes sounds like fiction because it is filled with drama.

The "Strictly Informative" Talk. This is the most common style of talk. It is also the most impersonal. Rarely does the speaker use the words *I* or *you*. He is more likely to refer to *they* when talking about people. Or to *them* or *it* when discussing the facts. The speaker is like an objective reporter telling facts. Instead of using dramatic incidents as anecdotes, facts and often figures are used, along with case histories.

Define Your Purpose. Once you choose your subject, define your purpose, which means you must decide on a definite objective. In other words, ask yourself, "What point do I wish to make in my talk?" There is only one main point you will want to make, so keep your definite objective in mind when planning your talk. Don't let your audience miss the point.

Another question to ask yourself: "Do I want to *tell* the audience something or do I want to *sell* them on an idea?" If there is one outstanding overall point you wish to tell them about, plan your talk around it. If there is an idea you would like to sell them on, build your speech around that point, making sure everything you say supports your definite objective. In that way, the audience will know that what you are saying is valid and be convinced by your presentation.

Choose Your Title. Now choose your title. Keep it as brief as possible, but also keep in mind that the purpose of a title is to attract attention. Titles that arouse curiosity are excellent, as they can draw an audience to a presentation. If the talk is to be informative, a title that highlights the main topic to be discussed is appropriate. An old trick used by professionals is to take a few words from the body of the talk and use them as the title. Amusing titles are also good, provided you have the ability to handle a talk that is amusing, humorous or light.

Use "You" Frequently. If you will be telling your own story by using the word *I* frequently, balance it by talking directly with the audience. This is easily done by using such phrases as "You might be interested to know..." or "If you want to try this, you should..."

You is the most popular word a speaker can use when talking to his or her audience. It keeps audiences' attention by involving them in what you are saying.

You Can Do It. Before you start preparing your talk, here are several important points to keep in mind:

What will you talk about in your talk? Choose that area of expertise that you feel most comfortable talking about.

Then talk about it in public.

Talk the same way you have been talking in private conversations, the way you most like to talk.

It is as easy as counting one-two-three.

SPEECHES—OR RATHER, TALKS—AND HOW TO PREPARE THEM

Next to stage fright, preparation of one's talk ranks highest on the list of tension-causers among inexperienced public speakers.

Preparing a talk, whether it is long or short, is easy when you know how to arrange your material.

Think of yourself as a person with a story to tell. The opening of your talk is like the front cover on a book. The ending is like the back cover. And that leaves your main talk as the pages in the book.

Choosing a Format. As a starter, you should know there are three categories, or formats, into which all talks fall. The type of format that is appropriate for your talk can probably be best determined by the type of event or program at which it is to be given.

The formats are: formal, semi-formal, and informal.

Mix and Match. There was a time when a speaker would not think of delivering an informal talk at a formal event, nor would a formal speaker dream of talking at an informal gathering. In today's eclectic mix and match world, however, anything and everything goes.

If you are in doubt as to the type of program at which you will be talking and you would feel more comfortable structuring your talk to the formality or informality of the specific program, confer with someone who knows. Usually the program chairman, department chairman, or host and hostess can answer your questions. Also, public relations people are great sources of advice.

If in doubt, do not hesitate to ask.

Now, let's look at the formats into which most talks fall.

The Formal Speech. When is a speech not a talk? There are times when a talk is not appropriate, but a speech is. There is a formal style for specific situations. This style is not for beginners. The strictly formal style involves pomp, circumstance, protocol and rigid adherence to rules. There isn't much room for creativity or off-the-cuff spontaneity. The speeches are written. These normally would not be given by a beginning speaker.

A strictly formal speech even might include any kind of ceremony or rite that follows an unbendable, inflexible outline. If an original speech is sandwiched between ritual, its style usually conforms to the general format of the event. Such a strictly formal event might take place in Buckingham Palace in a traditional ceremony in which an individual is knighted or a new monarch is installed on the throne.

Our American version of the formal event is exemplified in the President's Inauguration Ceremony or his State of the Union Message—with certain exceptions.

Formality, American Style. Americans are by nature outgoing, flexible people who are warm, generous and have senses of humor. Our fiercely won independence reflects in the way we talk with each other. We are open, honest and expressive. While we may appreciate tradition, we also bend it to suit our independence of spirit.

Despite the formality of the Presidential office, the individuals elected to that office are American-born citizens who reflect their individuality. Seldom is a President so rigid that he doesn't smile, or so stodgy that a glimmer of his own personality doesn't creep into his public addresses.

Not all presidents have had the stage presence of a Ronald Reagan. President Truman was known as "give 'em hell Harry" because he spoke in public with passion. Lyndon B. Johnson bared a surgical scar in a private place to the public.

Ronald Reagan earned the admiration of millions of Americans during his first presidential campaign because of an open, honest remark that ran uncensored in the press. In a moment of unexpected informality, Reagan shouted at a heckler, "Aw, shut up." His popularity soared overnight.

So, what is a formal speech, American style? Does it follow an antiquated tradition, or does it fit a uniquely modern format? It is actually structured to follow an outline and frequently contains an economy of meaningful words.

American-style formal speeches are seldom delivered spontaneously or "off- the-cuff" because most formal presentations require careful preparation.

A speech whose sole purpose is to impart data and specific facts may be best-suited to the formal approach, particularly if fitted into the framework of a tight time schedule that makes no allowance for audience participation.

Instances where the formal approach may be appropriate include installations; swearing-in and other rituals or ceremonies based upon tradition; business briefings by executives; business announcements of a public or private nature; formal social events based on rigid adherence to protocol; or matters involving state or national diplomatic affairs.

Because formal speeches are the most inflexible of all speech formats, formal speakers sometimes memorize their talks or read preedited discourses so their deliveries are word perfect.

A Semi-Formal Speech or Talk. The semi-formal approach, like the knee length evening gown instead of the ankle-length formal or the dark business suit worn in lieu of black tie and tux for social affairs, is highly acceptable in most instances that fall midway between "strictly formal" and "informal."

Semi-formal speaking combines the best of formal and informal formats, so the two speech styles can co-exist on the same program—and sometimes in the same talk.

An example is the chief executive of a corporation who delivers his/her message to the annual meeting of shareholders in formal format. Later, the floor is opened to discussion, and he/she answers stockholders' questions in an informal manner, by sticking to facts, but not to a script.

Panels of speakers at legal, scientific and medical symposia presenting abstracts related to business, research, and development often deliver their speeches according to the formal format, but join in informal Question and Answer sessions following their presentations.

Business meetings conducted by civic, social, educational, cultural, philanthropic and religious organizations run many programs successfully according to the semi-formal format. They follow the generally established outline of a program but allow informal discussions and talks to be given within the organized structure.

Seminars, classes and workshops of every conceivable kind are also successfully conducted according to the semi-formal format.

The Informal Talk. The informal format is everything the formal and semi-formal formats are not. And that leaves a pretty broad field.

Since most beginning public speakers speak informally, you probably won't have to be too concerned about preparing a formal word-perfect talk. But even the most informal talk should follow a basic outline.

The outline given here is equally adaptable to the formal, semi-formal and informal formats. The method by which it is delivered is the factor that will distinguish one style from another.

In the informal format, all that is required is that you jot down on a 3"x 5" note card the highlights of the material you plan to discuss. Then talk about it in your own words, as they flow, just as you would talk if you were in a private conversation with a friend.

The Sequence of Your Talk. Beginning speakers don't always know how to organize a talk so that it holds an audience captive. The following suggested sequential organization for the body of your talk should help simplify your outline and enable you to keep your audience interested from beginning to end.

- First, tell the history of your topic. How did you get into it? How did it begin? Flash back to the past. Give its background.

- Build toward the present by talking about your topic as it progressed from the past to the present moment. Use examples, illustrations and narrative, as suggested above. "An example is ..." "An illustration is ..."

- Bring your listeners up to the present moment. What is happening with your topic now? How can they benefit from it? How might it apply to them? How does it affect mankind? Or you? What significance does it have now?

Talk Outline. There are three basic parts to any talk, and each section plays a special role in making the overall talk complete. By using the blueprint given below as a guideline, you can easily adapt your talk, regardless of its length, to fit your needs.

The Opening. The opening is two-fold. Its purpose is to serve as an introduction, and it can usually be given in one or two short sentences of between 15 and 30 words total.

- Introduce yourself. Say a few words about how or why you came to be in the speaker's spotlight. Or acknowledge your host or hosts, if it is appropriate to do so. Or greet the audience by saying, "Ladies and gentlemen" or "Friends..."

- If there are any special instructions, such as inviting the audience to participate or asking them not to take pictures or tape record the talk, make your announcement in your introduction.

- If you want your audience to hold its applause, say so now. If there will be a Question and Answer session following your talk, this is the time to state that.

The purpose of the opening is to tell your audience what to expect.

The Middle. The public speaker is like a storyteller who uses the middle portion of his/her speech to tell his/her story. So once you have made your introduction, get right into the body of your talk.

You may use examples and illustrations throughout the body of your talk. Illustrations can be given as lists of data or significant facts and figures that enhance the topic. Visual aids such as blackboards, printed matter, videotapes or slides are used by many speakers to add depth to their presentation. If you are up to it, mix dramatic incidents with narrative to keep your audience attentive throughout your talk.

The Ending. The ending of your talk, like its opening, should be brief and serve a dual purpose:

- Summarize your talk by stating in a few words what you have been discussing.

- Conclude by recommending that your audience take action, if there is any to be taken. If there is no action to be taken, give your own personal opinion, based on your sincere conviction, about what the future holds for the topic you have discussed, or use an appropriate quotation.

- If there is to be a Question and Answer period, hold it after your concluding statement.

When your allotted time is up, thank your listeners for participating, end your presentation, and sit down.

How Much Can You Say In A Given Time? Always find out how much time has been allotted for your talk. Most speakers are given a specific length of time for delivering their talks, and they are advised beforehand. If you are to be a keynote speaker, plan to talk anywhere from fifteen to thirty minutes, which is the range of most keynote speeches. The average talk, however, lasts five minutes to thirty minutes. Few people can sit comfortably through a talk longer than thirty minutes. After you have talked over your topic with friends and associates, roughly time your talk. Practice several times with a timer or stopwatch.

If a Question and Answer period is scheduled, a basic rule of thumb is "one minute per question." When planning your talk, allow approximately one-fourth of your allotted time for your Q&A. After you have deducted that time, plan your talk around the remaining minutes given to you. For instance, if you have a thirty minute time slot, plan to speak for twenty-two or twenty-three minutes and hold a seven-minute Q&A, during which approximately seven questions will be discussed.

If talking a long time is not for you, consider an alternate type of presentation. After a short introduction, inform your listeners that you want to know what interests them most and that the remaining time is theirs to ask questions. Fielding questions from the audience not only takes some pressure off of you but gets the audience involved. Audience participation is fun and generates enthusiasm. It also allows you to be more concise with what you have to say.

Drafting Your Talk. After you have decided which style of talk you will give, draft your talk on note cards. As a beginner, be sure to stick to one style so your talk is consistent all the way through. In other words, don't start out with a first person account of your own true life experience and then switch to a "strictly informative" approach.

And don't get halfway through a strictly informative talk and then turn it into a how-to-do-it piece.

If, while you are drafting your talk, you feel you have turned a wrong corner or are trapped somewhere in the middle, you may have switched talk styles. Analyze your draft and get back on the main track. You will know you have accomplished this when your talk feels right.

How can you tell if your talk feels right? Simple. The talk will flow. One point will lead into another—as easily as counting one-two-three.

Practicing Your Talk. Practice your talk by imagining yourself already standing on the stage, looking out at your audience and saying what you plan to say.

Practice by yourself and in front of a friend. Pretend your friend is an entire audience—the audience you will be facing when you actually give your talk. If you wish, use a tape recorder or a camcorder to hear and/or see yourself.

Use note cards that contain the highlights you will be discussing, but try not to write out your talk. Just practice talking about the points you wish to make.

It is a good idea to time yourself. If you tend to run too long on one subject, cut it down. If another point needs embellishing, add something to it.

Practice until you get the "feel" of what you are talking about. When you feel it, it becomes natural to you, so natural that you will sound as if you are engaged in a private conversation with your public audience. In fact, talk about parts of your talk with friends and associates, weaving your material in until it is familiar and natural to you.

It is really so simple. All you have to be is *you*.

Examples of 12 Common Types of Talks

Whether your talk is formal, semi-formal or informal, or as brief as thirty seconds or as long as one-half hour, the basic outlines given here will help you organize it properly. Beginners in public speaking, or talking in public, may panic at the thought of presenting the routine or ordinary types of talks. By studying the following examples, which contain detailed guidelines about how to prepare the most common types of talks, you should be able to organize your own talk as easily as one-two-three—in other words, by its opening, middle, and ending.

The examples are listed alphabetically and not in the order in which they should be scheduled during a program. An example of a Question and Answer Session is given at the end.

The Acceptance Talk—The purpose of the acceptance talk is to accept an honor, a gift, or an office to which one has been named. It should be kept short and sincere. Look at the person giving the gift, not at the audience, while noting the following points in the order listed:

- Give thanks for what you have received.

- If you know what the gift is, mention it by name and tell why you are glad to receive it.

- Turn to the audience and thank the group for making it possible.

- Express best wishes for the success of the group.

Following is an example of an acceptance talk, which should generally be about as long as the presentation talk:

> Thank you for this most unexpected surprise. I thought maybe the company would give me a gold watch, but the trip for Mary and me to China leaves me speechless. You may not know that I was born in China. My parents were missionaries there when I was a baby. I don't remember it, but I have always wanted to see where I was born. Thanks to all of you who made this dream come true. Good wishes to you all.

The After Dinner Talk—The purpose of the after dinner talk is to entertain the audience. Whether it is simply a light, good-humored talk or a very informative business or professional talk, every after dinner talk should have a point to it.

The after dinner talk is generally the highlight of the program and, therefore, is often called a "keynote" talk.

The Announcement Talk—Both spoken and written announcements follow a pattern called "The 5 W's" of journalism, with the information to be given in the following order, or transposed but including the following major points:

Who   *What*   *When*   *Where*   *Why*   *(or how)*

Examples:

> John Jones, president of the Literary Club, will give a talk on Gutenberg Bibles on Saturday, June 3, at 7:30 P.M. in the Benjamin Franklin Library, located at 100 South Main Street. This is a fund-raising event. Proceeds will go toward repainting the library walls damaged during the fire in April. Donation is $10 for adults and $5 for children.

The first two points, the *Who* and *What*, can be interchanged. If a particular individual is spotlighted, use the name first. If an event is more significant than the speaker, use the event first, as follows:

> "Gutenberg Bibles" will be the topic of a talk to be given by John Jones, President of the Literary Club, on Saturday, June 3, at 7:30 P.M. in the Benjamin Franklin Library, located at 100 South Main Street. This will be a fund-raising event, with proceeds going for repainting of the library walls which were damaged by fire in April. Donations are $5 for children and $10 for adults.

If you wish to stress an important fact and be sure the audience doesn't forget it, state that fact at the beginning of your announcement and again at the ending. Be sure to include all the 5 "W's."

> Next Monday night, September 22, at 7:30 p.m., there will be a lecture on "Public Speaking" at the Monroe High School gymnasium. This lecture is of great importance be-

cause the speaker will be James Smith, a well-known authority on speech. There is no admission charge. Remember, it will be next Monday night at 7:30 P.M.

The Closing Talk—When the program is over, after all the questions and answers are ended and all announcements made, a simple closing comment concludes the gathering. Some speakers use their own words. Others like to end with a famous person's quotation that highlights or emphasizes the main purpose of the talk. Just a few words are all that is necessary. Keep the closing talk short, sweet, and to the point.

> That's it for this month. Thanks for coming. We'll see you all at the same time, same place, next month.

Another way of putting it is:

> That's all folks. There isn't any more.

The Farewell Talk—The purpose of the farewell talk is to say goodbye and, when appropriate, to convey thanks. The length of the farewell talk depends upon the occasion at which it is to be given and the time slot allowed for the talk.

Many farewell talks are delivered around a banquet table or at a retirement party, and are kept brief. They have three basic parts:

- To express regret (or happiness) at leaving and to thank those who have been closest to you

- To tell something about where you are going and what you plan to be doing

- To leave best wishes with the group

Two examples of the farewell talk are as follows; the first fairly long because it is being given to friends; the second short because it is more formal and impersonal:

> It is with mixed emotions that I stand here today, looking at the familiar faces of all of you with whom I have worked

for the last twelve years. There's Mary Jane, my faithful secretary, who was my right arm whenever there was a financial crunch. And Billy Lee, who was green behind the ears when he first came into the department straight out of high school and who labored faithfully by day at his duties while spending seven years at night school to get his degree. I can't think of anyone more deserving than Billy to take my place.

As some of you know, photography is my hobby. Alma and I are both shutterbugs, and we decided to take a year and travel around the country, shooting wildlife scenes in out-of-the-way places. We're going to try for some magazine covers. Maybe even do some creative writing to go along with the photos.

So I leave with mixed emotions. I will miss all of you who are more than just co-workers. You have become true friends. But I'm eager to experience the new freedom ahead. In fact, I haven't felt this way since I was a kid. So thanks, and best wishes to you all. And when we get back, I'll invite you all over so you can see the slides we've taken.

Here is an example of a more formal farewell talk, far more impersonal than the one just given:

I bid you farewell, not because it was my choice but because, as you all know, the economic downturn made it necessary to close this plant permanently.

You have all been faithful employees, and because of your hard work and dedication, I wish to present each of you with a severance check equal to two weeks' salary.
Some of you have asked about my own future. As you know, my father started this firm and I came behind him. I suppose I shall do something I've never done before. Look for a job.

Goodbye everyone. Thank you all. May God be with you.

Introduction of Speaker—The purpose of this talk is to introduce a speaker who will address the audience from the platform. The order in which the introductory talk is given is as follows

- Name the occasion

- Name the speaker, giving full name and title.

- Announce the subject. If there is a title, say it now.

- State the speaker's qualification to speak on the subject.

- Tell the position the speaker holds.

- Name any books he/she has written.

- Name any offices he/she has held.

- Turn the program over to the speaker and sit down.

An introductory talk should not ramble. If a speaker is very accomplished, instead of giving lists of his/her achievements, select a few pertinent key ones to announce. Neither the audience nor the speaker likes to be bombarded with laudatory phraseology.

Here is an example of an introductory talk:

> The Writers' Circle of Madison University is pleased to welcome Willie Rose to our monthly poetry readings. The title of his talk is "Iambic Pentameter in the Twentieth Century." He is currently an undergraduate student majoring in Elizabethan literature. Most of us know him from the Student Union, where he works part-time as cashier. Willie is currently working on his first book of poems, and he promises to share a few of them with us today. Some of our newer members may not be aware that it was Willie who started this group three years ago when he suggested that people who like poetry make themselves known.
> Welcome, Willie.

When the speaker has concluded, a short talk of thanks should be given, as follows:

Thank you for a most inspiring talk, Willie. I'm sure we all look forward to seeing your book in print next spring, and we will want you to autograph it personally for us.

The Master of Ceremonies—The master of ceremonies, or "Emcee," is in charge of the program's presentation. While an Emcee is not actually giving a talk, per se, he/she is nevertheless speaking before an audience. The Emcee must know what is going on during the program, because he/she is responsible for informing those assembled about it. Therefore, there are a few key points you should keep in mind if you are going to be an Emcee:

- You are presenting the show, not yourself.

- You should obtain a copy of the program well ahead of time and study it thoroughly to be familiar with the presentation of events.

- Check with the program chairman for any last minute changes to the program.

- Arrange the parts of the program to lead to the climax, or high point, so the main part doesn't happen too soon. (This is called *pacing*.) An audience does not like to sit around after the climax has been delivered, so plan the program to end shortly after the main event.

- If you are working with note cards, take extra cards and pencils. You may find that you must do some last minute revisions of the program. Leave a space between lines on your note cards for possible unplanned changes.

The Emcee opens and closes the program. He/she tells the audience why they are assembled and what is going to happen. If musicians are part of the program, he/she welcomes them. If there is an accompanist, he/she gives that person's name.

If the main portion of the program features a keynote speaker, he turns the program over to the individual who will introduce the main speaker. Some programs feature entertainment after the main speaker has talked.

When the performance is over, the Emcee thanks the person or persons who entertained. If it is a musical program, he/she may permit only one encore.

If there are any announcements to be made, the Emcee makes them now, following which he/she thanks the committee heads who put the event together.

Should any awards be given, the Emcee turns the program over to the individual who will be presenting the awards. The Emcee never presents awards personally.

The Emcee leads the applause and ends the program.

The importance of an Emcee cannot be underestimated. Without him/her, the program won't go on. If you are assigned the Emcee's role, the following tips will help you put on a program that goes smoothly, instead of surprising you with unexpected happenings such as a non-working loud speaker system or insufficient lighting for the speaker to read his note cards.

Plan to arrive at the event a half hour early. Let the chairman of the event know you are there. Note the size of the hall or room, then check to be sure the sound system is turned on and working. Check the volume to determine that it is neither too soft nor too loud.

Check the lighting on the platform and in the room. If it is not sufficient, arrange to have more lighting or stronger lights installed. Also check the room temperature and make adjustments if it is too hot or too cool.

Mingle with the audience as they arrive. Talk to people and listen to them. You may incorporate a comment or two from your conversation in your remarks. Start your program on time.

As I mentioned earlier, as Emcee you will be in charge of pacing the program. Another way of saying this is: you will be in charge of working out the program's routine.

It is best to avoid cliches in your presentation. Cliches are time worn phrases that everyone has heard too many times. They aren't fresh or sparkling. So, do not say such phrases as, "without further ado I give you Johnny Carson." Sometimes a simple hand gesture will indicate that you are presenting the speaker. Or a few fresh words of your own will convey the idea. Instead of saying, "It gives me great pleasure to present Sally Smith" it is much better to simply say, "I am happy to present Sally Smith."

While we are on the subject of cliches, avoid telling the audience, "I know you all will be interested in hearing the speaker tonight." Chances are, not all will be interested. Let the attendees decide for themselves after they have heard the speaker.

Because the Emcee's role is so flexible—it may be long or short, complicated or relatively simple—there is no single talk sample which will show you what an emcee should say. An Emcee may only open and close a program, leaving most of the other speeches to various members of the program committee; or, he/she may do most of the talking, except that of the keynote speaker or entertainment.

The Nomination Talk—The purpose is to nominate a candidate for office or position. Basic components of the nomination talk are:

- Mention the office for which the candidate will run or is being considered, and give the candidate's name.

- Present the requirements of the office, such as education, experience in the field, good health, honesty, friendliness, ability to get along well with others, specific skills.

- Show briefly how the candidate meets each of the above-stated requirements.

The following example shows how a candidate for office is presented:

Ladies and gentlemen, I nominate Marilyn Adams for the office of treasurer of the Art Guild. The treasurer's office requires an individual who has a background both in finances and fine arts, one who doesn't mind hard work and who has the stamina necessary to balance the budget and even raise funds, someone with honesty and the ability to work in harmony with other volunteers. In short, Marilyn Adams. Marilyn received her degree in Art History from UCLA. She has worked as a curator of several art museums and also is a Certified Public Accountant. Marilyn helps her husband in his own private business during tax season.

She has been a Cub Scout den mother and president of the

PTA, and now that her children are grown, she is eager to get back into the world of art on a voluntary basis. I urge you to vote for Marilyn.

An employee, presenting the name of a qualified candidate for promotion, might talk to his/her boss in this way:

I would like to recommend Steven Wilson for the comptroller's position. It requires someone who is excellently trained in the new tax reform laws and how they impact the company, and who is flexible enough to firm up last year's books while training his people in the new accounting procedures necessitated by the change in law.

Steven Wilson is one of the most mild-tempered people in the firm, and his knowledge of tax codes is outstanding. He pulled us out of a hole last year. He has been an excellent auditor, and he gets along well with the others in the department. Pressure doesn't get him down, and neither does change. He goes with it instead of resisting it. I think he is the candidate for the comptroller's position.

The Presentation Talk—If awards or gifts are to be given out, they should be presented after the keynote speaker has finished.

The structure of a presentation talk is as follows:

• State the occasion

• Note the gift being awarded.

• State name of recipient

• Mention the reason the gift or award is being given.

• Offer a few words of praise to the recipient, then hand him or her the object.

• Express good wishes to the recipient.

As an example, a gift, given to an individual retiring from a company after many years of service, is presented using this format:

At this farewell luncheon for Jonathan Rigby, who has been with Electrical Controls for 25 years, the officers and fellow employees of the tax department join together in presenting John with something he has always wanted, a pair of round-trip tickets to China. John, you always said someday you would like to spend your vacation on the Great Wall, and no one deserves to have his dreams come true more than you do. It has been wonderful working with you.

We hope you and Mrs. Rigby enjoy yourselves and we wish you the very best in the future.

The Toast—A toast, honoring a person, is a special kind of talk that has a specific structure:

- Name the occasion.

- Tell what the person has done.

- Tell why he/she deserves something special.

- Note the purpose of the toast.

The speaker giving a toast should be standing. If the audience is seated, he/she should ask the audience to also stand.
Example:

At this meeting of the Dramatic Club, I would like to recognize a person who has been in this group for several years. He has not been in the limelight, but he has still worked very hard behind the scenes. He has directed some of our most successful plays and yet has not received enough credit. He is a wonderful person, always willing to help out, and always in the right place at the right time.

Will you please rise and drink a toast with me to Dave Johnson.

The Welcome Talk—The purpose of the welcome talk is to welcome special guests. There are two basic kinds of welcome talks:

- **Welcome Everyone.** Everyone is greeted and the name of the event or special occasion is mentioned.

- **Special Guest.** Special guests are welcomed by name. Also noted are the names of their organization(s), along with the guests' outstanding accomplishments, if any.

Here are examples of the two basic kinds of welcome talks:

Welcome everyone to the 25th reunion of the Class of 1965. As I look over this great turnout, I can see that none of us has changed a bit. (Pause for audience reaction.)

We are fortunate to have with us some of our former teachers. We are glad to welcome Kathy Arnold, Jeannie Jones and William Broderick. Your influence on our lives has been tremendous. We are so happy you could celebrate with us today.

The Question and Answer Session—The Question and Answer portion of a program, best known as the Q&A, can be as important as the talk itself. During the Question and Answer period, the audience participates by asking questions and making comments, and the speaker usually acts as a moderator.

If you plan to let your audience participate in your presentation, inform your listeners in the opening of your talk. You may say:

"Ladies and gentlemen, if you have any questions during my presentation, please raise your hands."

Or. . .

"After my talk there will be a short Question and Answer period. So save your questions and comments until then please."

Yet another way of handling a Q&A, especially if you want to screen the questions rather than take them as they come, is to say:

"If you have any questions, please write them on a piece of paper and hand them to me after I've concluded my talk."

People are sometimes reluctant to be the first to make a comment, to ask a question or even to raise a hand. If no one comes forward to kick off your Question and Answer session, pick out a person near you in the audience, look at him or her and ask:

"Is there anything I didn't cover that you would like to know about?"

Or. . .

"Have you ever had a similar experience to the one I discussed?"

This usually leads into a discussion. If, however, no one is yet ready to start talking, ask for a show of hands and ask:

"How many of you here found the topic interesting?"

When the hands go up, call on someone close to you in the audience and offer this question:

"Would you care to tell us what interested you?"

Once one person breaks the ice, your Q&A will be under way.

A rich variety of information can be exchanged during a Q&A. People add what they know about a subject and the speaker can learn as much as the audience. If someone asks a question to which you don't know the answer, handle it by saying:

"Is there anyone here who wishes to comment on the question?"

Or, if no one knows the answer, including you, handle the situation graciously by saying:

"I'm sorry, but I can't answer that. But it certainly deserves looking into."

You may come across people who talk a lot whenever they get the chance. These people like to dominate a Q&A session. Sometimes they are loudmouths who talk for the sake of talking, whether or not they have anything meaningful to contribute.

At the first opportune moment, break into a loudmouth's comments and simply thank him or her. Then either make a remark about the person's comments, ask someone else to give a response, or go on to the next question.

Once a Q&A takes off, it is likely to keep right on going. But time limits prevent endless open discussion. No two questions or answers are exactly the same length. Many speakers plan on taking five questions during a five minute Q&A period, allowing one per minute, according to plan. Some questions lend themselves to greater response and commentary. Others can sometimes be answered with one or two simple words.

As a speaker, you will have to watch the clock, and when only one minute is left for your Q&A, ask for your last question. You might even be able to squeeze in two questions during that time slot.

When your time limit is about up, announce:

"I can take one more question."

Then take that question only. Even if a dozen hands are waving, say courteously:

"Sorry, we have run out of time."

Thank everyone for their participation and end your presentation.

A final note about the Q&A: I find that many beginning speakers are very comfortable with Q&A, since it is similar to the give and take of normal conversation. The Q&A moves the spotlight from the speaker and is a natural way of providing information. I would say that the Q&A is the best and simplest way for beginning speakers to learn to talk in public.

SPOTLIGHT ON SPEAKING

Once you become involved in talking in public, you will want to learn all you can about it. The following are a few guidelines that will help you along the way.

Be observant. Watch TV and listen to the radio. Observe the hosts, but don't try to imitate them. Listen to talk show guests—they are also public speakers—and especially listen to and watch public speakers giving a talk or speech on TV.

Attend programs featuring speakers. Join in Q&A sessions by speaking up.

Listen to teachers, clergymen, politicians, or members of the PTA giving committee reports. Play a little game with yourself by trying to tell which speakers have experience in public speaking and which ones do not.

> **Beginner's Mistakes.** Here are a few inappropriate responses that may be made by beginning speakers. Try to avoid these pitfalls.

> **Apologizing**—Sometimes if a speaker catches himself/herself in a mispronunciation or loses his/her train of thought, he/she apologizes, then backtracks and starts over. Don't apologize for your lack of experience as a speaker.

Praises—Don't overstate your praises of people at the event. Most individuals would rather be acknowledged less profusely, by a simple nod, handshake or more realistic introduction. Over-praising sounds phony.

Introductions—When introductions get so out of hand that a host introduces practically every person at the event, the program begins to get boring. The audience didn't come to hear a "Who's Who at the Banquet." They came to hear the featured speaker.

When introductions are overdone, it is unfair to the guest speaker because by the time it is his/her turn to talk, people have already heard enough. What it boils down to is that the host stole the show and bored the audience with his/her performance. Introductions should be short and to the point. Then the host should sit down.

Repetition—Beginning speakers sometimes belabor the same point by repeating it again and again. They need to learn that once is enough.

Thanking—Beginning speakers sometimes tend to overdo their thanks, or, conversely, forget their thanks entirely. A simple smile, nod, wave or handshake, or the words "thank you" are sufficient ways to convey a message of appreciation at both the beginning and ending of a talk.

Pauses—Beginning speakers often break up their sentences with pauses while they are trying to overcome initial stage fright, get their thoughts together, or think of what to say next.

Experienced speakers pause, too, but their pauses are part of the timing they have developed from speaking in public. They pause when a new topic is about to be introduced or when they want to let the audience absorb an idea they have imparted. They pause if a plane or ambulance passing outside makes a distracting noise, and they pause to let a person having a coughing spell quiet down.

A public speaker learns through experience to develop his/her own "metier" so that pauses and the rhythm of the talk make it more effective.

Meaningless Words—Beginning speakers sometimes fill their pauses with meaningless words such as "uh and well and er," "uh and like," and, "uh and you know."

Experienced speakers who may, at one time, have used these same talk habits in their conversations have eliminated them. They practice their conversational etiquette so often it comes naturally. And they seldom start a sentence with the word "Well" ...

Images—Beginning speakers often appear uptight, stiff and uncomfortable. They don't come across as warm, friendly, relaxed people because the images they project are unnatural.

Experienced speakers have learned that by being themselves, they project the best of all possible images: their natural selves.

Smiles—Beginning speakers don't always smile. They sometimes seem to be so serious their faces appear frozen, or their brows are so furrowed they seem shadowed.
Experienced speakers not only smile, they laugh if the mood calls for it. But they don't crack jokes unless they are good at humor and the occasion calls for it.

YOUR FUTURE AS A PUBLIC SPEAKER

After you have completed your first talk, there is a real chance you may leave the stage with the question already forming in your mind: "How can I further develop my public speaking abilities?"

The following suggestions will shed light on some ways you may wish to continue public speaking.

Join a Group. To start, join a group—any group that appeals to you, and in which you will have a chance to speak to people. It can be a church club or a civic or social organization such as the Lions Club, the Rotary Club or the Women's Club in your local area.

If you are a business person, it would be helpful to join one of the numerous businessmen's and businesswomen's organizations whose memberships consist of people in lines of work similar to yours. There are organizations for secretaries, accountants, nurses, doctors, and just about every profession.

Most of these groups are non-profit organizations whose officers are volunteers. Although they are not paid for their services, there are always plenty of committees comprised of volunteer groups.

Get on a committee. Volunteer to hold an office, even if you have never done so before. Then attend the meetings and speak up.

If your organization plans a benefit or a banquet or any other kind of program requiring the services of people who like to speak in public, volunteer to be on the program.

Get Involved in Politics. Another way to become active in public speaking activities is to join the local branch of your political party's support group. The behind-the-scenes activity is fascinating, and the discussions of issues and candidates, as well as the opportunity to meet and talk with elected officials, is stimulating. In such a group, you will have the chance to think on your feet and speak what is on your mind without rehearsing your talk. The more spontaneous, "off-the-cuff" speaking in public you do, the easier it becomes to make the switch to speaking in public **at ease** under any circumstance.

Sometimes you will be able to conduct public polls or work in the precinct polling place when elections are held. This will allow you to meet total strangers and practice speaking with the public.

Conduct Surveys or Market Research. If you live in a major metropolitan area, there are probably numerous firms in your town which conduct ongoing surveys or market research. Many of these firms operate at night, so if you hold a full time job, you might be able to squeeze one or two nights a week into handling a second position, which pays you for practicing your public speaking.

The ways these firms work vary with each organization and the kind of surveys being conducted, but two main types are:

Phone Surveys—There is no selling involved. People are contacted by phone and asked questions relating to products they use or TV shows they watch or what kind of funeral plots they prefer. The data is collected and turned over to the firm, which in turn compiles its findings into reports for the client that has hired it to conduct the research.

Public Polls—Again, no selling is involved. Public polling is often done outside of supermarkets or other shopping centers. People are asked if they have a few minutes to spend in answering a few questions. The answers are written down and turned into the firm. This is another way of practicing public speaking techniques on an in-person basis with total strangers.

Study Public Speaking. Many high schools, colleges and universities offer special courses for beginning speakers. It isn't necessary to be a full time student to enroll in these courses, which often are taught during evening hours in special adult education classes. But be sure such a course lets you practice speaking. If it only teaches theory from a book, forget it. In addition, there are numerous "self-help" organizations and private schools that teach specialized subjects such as public speaking.

Teach a Class. You don't have to hold a teaching credential to teach seminars and workshops, or classes in just about everything from home cooking to yoga relaxation techniques. All you need is familiarity with and experience in your subject.

Nor do you need to rent a classroom to conduct a learning session. Do it at home. Lots of others are inviting groups of people into their living rooms or garages, onto their patios or around their swimming pools, with the purpose of teaching short classes that may last only an hour or two.

All teachers, both public and private, are public speakers. And teaching a class is a great way to enjoy yourself, make friends and practice your public speaking.

If you are an expert at making chicken noodle soup from scratch with homemade noodles, you could teach cooking. If you have written a magazine article that has been published, teach your friends how they, too, can do creative writing. If you have built a notched shelf in your garage, using scrap wood that you have put together without nails, teach your friends how to do it, too.

If teaching interests you, you might inquire at schools in your area about the possibility of giving a seminar, workshop or series of special classes. Many specialized classes are taught by non-professional teachers who have expertise in everything from foreign languages to oil painting.

Remember, everyone is an expert at something. That means you, as well. (Maybe you are well-qualified to teach more than one subject.) If the thought of teaching appeals to you, just remember to teach about something you are very familiar with and truly enjoy personally.

Experience is Golden. Experience is the public speaker's most valuable asset. The more experience you gain, the more polished you will become as a public speaker; and the more polished you become, the more you will shine.

Developing your abilities in the ways outlined above gives you an excellent opportunity to work out the kinks every newcomer encounters when just starting out as a public speaker.

Don't be discouraged if you make mistakes. Learn from them, and try, try again.

Practice. Practice. Practice.

And keep it short, sweet and to the point. Shakespeare summed up this important idea when he wrote, "Brevity: the soul of wit."

Onward and Upward. Most public speakers never become paid professionals. But every professional public speaker began as an amateur. If you are one of the rare few who wants to progress beyond amateur status and step onto the stage as a professional public speaker, how can you continue moving onward and upward?

The Lecture Circuit. When you feel you are experienced—and your audiences applaud you on a consistent basis—you are ready to move on to the lecture circuit, either as an amateur or as a professional public speaker.

An amateur performs public speaking free of charge. The professional public speaker receives an honorarium or fee for making appearances.

Lecture circuit is a term that applies to a broad area in which public speakers appear at various types of functions. Generally, the speakers who are featured on the circuit are handled by speakers' bureaus.

Join a Speakers' Bureau. The function of the speakers' bureau is to handle the bookings of speakers for particular functions their clients are giving. Speakers' bureaus generally have a stable of public speakers upon whom they can call to fill clients' specialized needs.

If you feel you are ready to take your public speaking "on the road," consider joining a speakers' bureau. They are usually listed under S in the yellow pages of the phone book.

When you are part of a speakers' bureau team, you will have arrived as a seasoned public speaker.

You won't have to call them. They will call you.

ONE MORE TIME

Just follow this easy formula, and giving your talk will be as easy as one. . . two. . . three:

1. Open with a brief introduction in which you thank your host or hostess for inviting you to participate in the program. Briefly touch on what you will be talking about.

2. Tell your story. This is the body of your talk. Relate it as it happened to you. Use anecdotes, if you are comfortable and able, and illustrations or examples in your talk. Stick to details and facts that enhance your theme.

3. End your talk by wrapping up what you have been saying. In other words, summarize what you have said in a brief statement. Conclude your talk by addressing the audience. If you have a sales pitch, make it now. If you have any advice, give it now. If there is any kind of action you are inviting the audience to take, state it now. And if you are going to hold a question and answer session, open the floor to audience participation now. Then, after you have heard all the questions and comments time allows, thank the audience and sit down.

It is Revolutionarily Easy. Public speaking today is revolutionary because it is so open, and so easy.

If you enjoy holding private conversations, you will love public conversations. Because that is what today's public speaking is: private conversation made public.

You can do it. I know you can.

So, if you are ready, get set.

Go for it!

QUESTIONS & ANSWERS

Q: Should I memorize my talk?

A: Not unless the talk you are giving is part of a ritual or ceremony that requires word-perfect delivery that appears spontaneous. Otherwise, no. Memorized talks usually come across as unnatural, stiff and insincere.

It is all right to memorize short passages, such as quotes that you will include in your talk or facts that must be accurate, but keep them brief. Better still, have such material on 3"X 5" note cards, know it well, and read it off. That would save you the trouble of having to memorize it.

If you really want to learn to talk in public by thinking on your feet, do not memorize your talk.

Q: I've heard some people read their talks. They aren't Ronald Reagan. Is there another way of giving a talk?

A: There are several types of speakers: those who talk from a written script; those who ad lib or talk extemporaneously from notes; and those who talk impromptu or "off the cuff" without notes. I have seen those who write out their presentations and do very well. It takes a long time to do, but they have learned to do it, and they sound good.

Conversely, I like to chat from notes within my mind. I talk over the material long before I speak in public. I try it out in bits and pieces with different people in conversations everywhere until I am familiar with the material.

The type of presentation used depends upon the speaker and the occasion. For formal and important presentations, the written approach works best. For informal and free-flowing presentations which are the majority of talks, requiring give and take, I go with the "off the cuff" style.

Q: Should I use visual aids?

A: Yes, but only if artwork, slides, charts, graphs or other supplementary material will enhance your presentation or display important information the audience should know about. You may also use a blackboard or hand out samples of printed material to supplement your talk.

Q: What do you mean by being yourself when you talk in public?

A: Talk naturally, as if you are in private conversation with someone you are trying to understand and who is trying to relate to you. Don't be phony; don't be formal or different from the way you normally are. Don't look for big words or perfect ways to express yourself. Tension comes from trying to be someone you aren't, trying to impress, or trying to be perfect. Just be natural.

Q: What happens if my talk is too short?

A: If your talk is concluded sooner than you had planned, hold a Q&A even if you hadn't meant to do so. To kick it off, ask: "Does anyone have any comments or questions?"

Q: What is the best way to learn to talk in public?

A: Stand up and talk in public—again and again and again. Get feedback from your friends and people who have heard you talk. Record yourself on audio and video. See if you are direct and natural, conversational and organized. Be yourself. Don't try to perform. And practice, practice, practice. That is the only way.

Chapter 9

The World of Voice Disorders

THE DECLINE AND FALL OF THE AMERICAN VOICE

Greta Garbo, Ingrid Bergman, John Wayne and Joan Crawford are but a few of the names that come to mind when recalling great movie stars of the past. "They had faces then," say longtime movie fans. The fact is, they had *voices*, too.

Lauren Bacall is known not only for her sexy, sultry looks, but for an unmistakable voice that perfectly complements her appearance. Most of us believed that she was talking naturally with her husky, throaty voice. Today, I know better.

During the Golden Age of movies, the studios often tried to alter the voices of their stars. Lauren Bacall did not have her trademark sound when she first went to Hollywood. She explained in her autobiography, *By Myself*, that her voice was low, but that it tended to rise when she became nervous or emotional. Howard Hawks, her producer/director, didn't like what he heard. "Nothing is more unattractive than screeching," he told her. He insisted that she train her voice so that it would remain low at all times.

On her own Lauren Bacall drove into the nearby mountains where she read aloud from a book "in a voice lower and louder than normal." She changed her voice, but I understand she ultimately developed problems with it.

These days, people everywhere are abusing their voices by forcing an unnatural sound. They may know what they want in a voice, but they don't know how to get it.

Joan Rivers came to me when she developed problems with her voice. So did Anne Bancroft, Diahann Carroll, and Richard Crenna—stars who rely on their voices for their livelihood. O. J. Simpson said, "After just an hour with Dr. Cooper, I noticed a change in my voice, and I had a direction to go in."

Everyone wants to be a winner. For some, that might mean speaking in a masculine way or in a sexy way; others are after a voice that rings with authority and confidence. They not only want to sound impressive, they want to make a sound impression.

Confidence, authority, leadership, power, and desirability are just a few sought-after qualities that form images in our minds. Those images are often transferred to the voice, making us speak as we think a person should to achieve those qualities. Without proper guidance, however, the sound becomes forced and unnatural, resulting in damage to the vocal cords.

The seductive voice (bedroom voice) is often attractive, and has become the trademark of numerous celebrities. Marilyn Monroe used it. So did Jayne Mansfield, Hedy Lamarr, Lauren Bacall, James Mason, and Charles Boyer. To achieve a seductive voice, you simply drop the pitch and use little volume. The word breathy is often associated with it.

The seductive voice is not a voice to use constantly. Use it to make a point, then return to your natural voice. The seductive voice is highly effective for specific occasions, primarily because of its confidential and intimate tone, but often a misdirected lowered voice with reduced volume can irritate the vocal folds and create voice problems if used over a long period of time.

Gershon M. Lesser, M.D., a highly respected internist in Los Angeles, believes the voice is a "second face," representing us through speech and sound. As a diagnostician, Dr. Lesser finds three-fourths of his patients complaining of sinusitis, post-nasal drip and allergy really have voice problems but don't know it. They experience tired voice, morning voice, failing or troubled sound, laryngitis, hoarseness, and so on. "Their problems stem from speaking incorrectly," states Dr. Lesser.

Dr. Lesser experienced a voice problem while hosting a weekly radio show, *The Health Connection*. Faced with the option of surgery or voice rehabilitation, Dr. Lesser chose voice rehabilitation. I had the opportunity to work with Dr. Lesser and helped him regain his voice. His theory is, "You can always *do* a surgery, but you can't *undo* it." Dr. Lesser is a leading advocate of self-help methods. His concluding comment was: "Before you think of surgery, think of Dr. Cooper's 'magic' cure; it even astounds the doctors."

The sound revolution has played a major role in the decline and fall of the American voice. We know we don't sound good, or at least as good as we'd like to sound, so we squeeze and mash our voices. As a result, our voices tire and fail, become hoarse, or give us trouble by fading in and out. We clear our throats and cough. We look for a remedy to cure "outside influences." All too often, the problems are self-inflicted.

Talking can be fun and exciting, but not with a voice that is misused.

TROUBLED AND PROBLEM VOICES

When I was a guest on the TV show, *Hour Magazine*, Gary Collins asked his studio audience if anyone had trouble with his/her voice. (Collins had told me before we went on the air he did not believe very many people had troubled voices.) To his surprise, quite a few hands were raised.

The number was actually relatively low, since many people have voice problems without realizing it. The majority of the people who complain about sinusitis, allergies, and post-nasal drip have troubled or problem voices; yet they fail to hear what their voices are saying about them. A troubled voice says you are down when you are up, angry when you are calm, blah when you are raring to go. A troubled voice says so much. It is talking *for* you, and yet it isn't. It is talking *to* you, but you can't hear it.

Every day, we hear troubled and problem voices resulting from voice misuse and abuse. They sound erratic and strange; the voices come and go. Among the most common types of troubled or problem voices are nasal voices, depressed or angry voices and, especially, tired voices.

You can have a tired voice at any age, but it occurs more and more as a person grows older. With lowered pitch (which can also denote despair, resignation, hostility) and poor breathing habits, the voice begins to falter and, at times, fails. The tone wavers and the volume decreases, affecting the carrying power. A person with a tired voice is frequently asked, "What did you say?"

Lovra, a retired machinist, suffered for years with a troubled voice that continually had people asking, "What did you say?" Whenever he wanted to meet someone, he could get through the introduction with a few words but he could not carry on a conversation. "I was a dead fish," he admits. What hurt Lovra even more was the reaction of his family and friends in his native Yugoslavia. At a family reunion three years ago, he was constantly told to speak louder. His elderly mother could not hear him at all.

When Lovra tried to speak up, he coughed, irritating his throat until it bled. Lovra blamed cigarettes even though he had given up smoking ten years ago.

Lovra's unhappy experience with his family prompted him to seek medical attention when he returned home. A highly recommended ENT specialist in Los Angeles cleaned out Lovra's ears and checked his throat before dismissing him. Lovra next saw a medical doctor in Beverly Hills. "Don't worry," the doctor told him, "you don't have cancer. You have an allergy." Lovra was instructed to stop eating peaches.

One evening, by chance, Lovra tuned to my cable television show. During the program, I demonstrated to a guest the "humming of America." Lovra watched closely, then tried humming himself. His voice was instantly stronger and louder. Encouraged, he set out to find a copy of *Change Your Voice, Change Your Life*, which had been mentioned during the telecast. "I read the book," said Lovra, "repeating the exercises over and over. It was so simple. A few words every day was all it took. And I didn't get any help from a medical doctor."

Today, Lovra no longer coughs. His bleeding is gone. His new, clear, stronger voice gives him approval and confidence. It goes on and on without fading or growing tired. He feels free to talk. People no longer ask him to repeat himself. And he eats peaches.

Most cases of voice tiredness are either ignored or merely acknowledged by physicians, who have little awareness that voice fatigue is but a symptom of voice misuse. Few referrals, I fear, are made to voice pathologists.

I have attempted all of my long career to bring the field of voice rehabilitation out of obscurity and to the attention of the public—to tell everyone that there is help for misused and abused voices, for voice disorders, and for people who want to improve their speaking voices.

I have used every means possible to publicize voice rehabilitation. I have written articles, chapters, and books. I have given thousands of radio and television interviews. I have made speeches and conducted seminars. I have presented patients at conferences and medical meetings for peer review. I have been fortunate that some celebrity patients I have helped have allowed me to use their names. I want this field to become vocally visible to the general public. Quietly doing voice rehabilitation and being successful will help a few, but in order to get many patients to seek help from professionals in this field, the field must be publicized.

What I am trying to tell the public is: "Look, if you want a better, more effective voice—or if you are losing your voice—here are simple, natural techniques that work. If you have a so-called troubled voice, and you have been to doctor after doctor without results, why not try something practical and conservative instead of surgery?" Chances are, you may find that your trouble ends.

While my field is saying that I cannot essentially analyze the voice in seconds, I am doing just that every day in my office, over the telephone on local and national radio shows, and on network and syndicated television. Many hosts of these shows, Larry King and Oprah Winfrey included, were at first skeptical. But they later inferred that I was a phenomenal being, which I am not. I am actually a journeyman with a good ear. Almost everybody has the same abilities that I have, and can do exactly what I am doing if only they want to learn. That is because the techniques are so very simple.

Remember, *finding* your natural voice often takes seconds. Learning to use it with proper mid-section breath support takes time and training. The natural voice must be automatic in various situations and with different people.

SPASTIC DYSPHONIA

The most devastating of the voice disorders is spastic dysphonia—the strangled voice trapping the person in silence.

I liken spastic dysphonia to constant stage fright. Everyone knows what far-reaching effects stage fright has on a speaker. That's because there is a chemical and neurophysiological change affecting the adrenaline flow of the body when an individual talks in public, as compared to private conversation. Spastic dysphonics, I find, have perennial stage fright. They are forever afraid of talking, fearing they cannot talk well.

Many doctors find spastic dysphonia to be an irreversible neurological problem. I believe spastic dysphonia is a mechanical voice problem with psychological overtones. The individual with the condition is talking with the brakes on. Not realizing what they are doing, the problem continues.

When I was on the staff and later a clinical assistant professor on the medical faculty at UCLA Medical Center from 1960 to 1969, we never had one success using extensive interdisciplinary services with spastic dysphonia. But as a single practitioner in private practice, I have had successes for the past twenty years with spastic dysphonia using Direct Voice Rehabilitation.

In 1982, at Cedars-Sinai Medical Hospital, Los Angeles, I presented three patients who had confirmed severe spastic dysphonia to an audience of Ear, Nose and Throat doctors. These patients told the audience how they had recovered their speaking voices by Direct Voice Rehabilitation. Dr. Henry J. Rubin, a well-known ENT specialist, asked after the presentation: "We know that you are the only one successful by speech therapy. Why?" The answer is, I do not do speech therapy. I do Direct Voice Rehabilitation. Henry J. Rubin, M.D., Associate Professor, Department of Head and Neck Surgery, UCLA School of Medicine, Retired, and Former Chief of the Service of Otolaryngology, Cedars of Lebanon Hospital, Los Angeles, commented in 1990: "In the fifteen years immediately preceding my retirement from the active practice of otolaryngology, I referred my patients in need of voice rehabilitation to Dr. Cooper because his results proved to be the most consistently satisfactory. His methods seemed essentially to be quite simple, in fact to the point sometimes of challenging believability, but they worked. He explains these methods in his book, and I believe that any voice therapist who gives them a serious and unbiased trial will be agreeably surprised."

In 1990, I returned as a guest speaker at Cedars-Sinai Medical Center. This time I presented five patients with diagnosed spastic dysphonia and discussed how I had helped them with Direct Voice Rehabilitation. Regarding the treatment of spastic dysphonia by Direct Voice Rehabilitation in patients seen in his private practice group, a very prominent otolaryngologist, Edward A. Kantor, M.D., Chairman, Division of Otolaryngology, Head and Neck Surgery, Cedars-Sinai Medical Center, Los Angeles, had this to say: "Dr. Morton Cooper has shown unusual expertise in treating patients with spastic dysphonia. His methods of voice therapy in our patients afflicted with this markedly disabling disease have been highly successful."

The only way I know to call attention to the fact that spastic dysphonia may be helped by Direct Voice Rehabilitation is to let patients who have recovered from spastic dysphonia tell their stories. In this way I have hoped that other voice pathologists will help other patients. Remember, these are real stories about real people; only their first name was used to protect their privacy.

Most recently, a patient named Donald visited my office. Donald had severe spastic dysphonia for forty years. Doctors at a well known medical center in the Midwest had told him ten years ago that his condition was hopeless, and they suggested psychological help. Five years later, a speech pathologist said he could do nothing to help Donald, but that he should try surgery. Donald refused. He didn't want surgery or botulinum then, nor did he want it when he came to see me, at age 73.

I started Donald on my Instant Voice Press. At first his voice sounded squeezed, barely there at all. But within ten minutes, Donald had his real voice back. After all these years, he heard himself speak again. He was more than delighted. Said Donald, "On a scale of one to ten . . . ten being the best . .

To repeat: finding the natural voice is not difficult nor time-consuming; learning to use and maintain the natural voice requires time and cooperation.

Many spastic dysphonic cases I've worked with were extremely severe. A number come with medical diagnoses from leading medical centers throughout the United States, including UCLA Medical Center, the Mayo Clinic, and Stanford University. For example, in a *Los Angeles Times* article written by Beverly Beyette, she reports:

> Dr. Don Dodson started having voice problems 10 years
> ago and was diagnosed at Stanford University as having

spastic dysphonia, probably incurable. "I was finally discharged after being told they'd done everything they could," he said.

Dodson, who is assistant vice president, academic affairs, University of Santa Clara, remembered reading a Morton Cooper book and sought him out. "It took me a year of working with him to really catch on to the techniques," Dodson said, "and another two years to work them into everyday speech." Today, he said, it is an automatic response—"If I find myself starting to slip into the lower throat, I'll try to hop back up." And the spasticity has not returned.*

People come to me from all over the world to get help. Professor Fereydoon, who came from Iran, made the following statement on September 9, 1989:

In 1973, because of laryngitis and vocal misuse due to my career as Professor at the University, my vocal cords gradually became weak in such a way that I could hardly speak. In the beginning, I contacted an Ear, Nose and Throat doctor in Tehran and he gave me antibiotics to use. I did not get better and in summer 1973 I went to England in order to see a voice therapist. This trip was of no use and my problem became worse.

In summer 1974, I went to the United States and consulted my cousin who, as a medical pathologist, was making research at Rutgers Medical School at that time. She said that I should first see Dr. F. and if his treatment might not be useful, I should go to Los Angeles in order to see Dr. Hans von Leden. Dr. F.'s prescription was funny, as he told me to chew a golf ball and for this matter one of my teeth broke apart.

In September 1974, I went to Los Angeles in order to see

*Beverly Beyette, "Therapist Talks Up Voice Makeovers," *Los Angeles Times,* 11 July 1984, p. 1 (View).

Dr. von Leden. He, for the first time, diagnosed my problem as Spastic Dysphonia and after extensive examinations referred me to Dr. Morton Cooper. . . .

On September 12, 1974, I saw Dr. Cooper in his office. He said that I suffered from Spastic Dysphonia and should undergo vocal rehabilitation. The length of time needed for the treatment was stipulated as 1 to 4 years in the initial session with the possibility that one year may be sufficient.

I stayed in Los Angeles from September 1974 to July 1975. During this period, I used to see Dr. Cooper . . . in the beginning a few times a week. His treatment was a new experience in my life as I regained my natural voice and also my career. In the beginning, I was pessimistic towards the outlook of the treatment, but after a few months, while exercising Dr. Cooper's methods and reading his book, I found out that my voice was going to its natural level without slipping back to a low level. I still remember Dr. Cooper's statement, namely: "Since you are a theoretician and teach economic theory, you would be able to learn the right methods of speaking."

This was proved, as his treatment became fully effective and after eleven months, I was back to my real voice, without losing ends of words and sentences.

Personally, I owe my regained natural voice to Dr. Cooper. I admire his patience and kindness. Of course, I worked very hard during the period of rehabilitation, exercising his methods of humming words first and later sentences and breathing correctly.

Finally, I have been able to teach regularly every semester since September 1975, carrying a full load of 15 hours per week on the average. Thanks to Dr. Cooper for his rehabilitation program.

Here is what a few other patients have to say:
Reverend Albert, Georgia:

Being a minister, I found myself frustrated. I had seen ten different doctors and received no help and very little encouragement. I had almost decided to take early retirement.
One day, while listening to WSB Radio in Atlanta, I heard Dr.
Cooper on a telephone talk show. I went home and called
him. . . .

After spending four days with Dr. Cooper in February 1989, I
realized that my voice was back. He taught me how to help
myself.

I will always be grateful.

Marjorie, California:

My sister-in-law, who is a teacher in Los Angeles, had cut
out an article in a teachers' magazine about a teacher Dr.
Cooper had cured of spastic dysphonia. My symptoms
were the same, so I decided that if she received help I could
also be helped.

I came to Dr. Cooper's office in October, 1987, in desperation. I was in so much pain from the top of my head down
to my middle back that I could hardly bear it, and I spoke
only in a broken whisper.

Dr. Cooper was like a light at the end of a very dark tunnel,
after seeing ten other doctors ranging from ear, nose and
throat specialists, psychiatrists, hypnotherapy, biofeed-
back therapy, psychotherapy, and finally acupuncture for
the severe pain. The last doctor at UCLA wanted to cut the
nerve to one of my vocal cords and I said, "No thanks," realizing that would not be the solution for me.

With the many months of daily therapy, I have learned to
breathe properly and to make the humming sound in the

mask of the face. These were essential before learning to speak at my natural pitch. I feel that my speaking voice is now 85 percent normal, and with continued therapy I have no doubt that my normal speaking voice will soon be restored.

The Reverend James, Illinois, who had had spastic dysphonia for nine years, tried all kinds of therapy for his voice problem, even going to the Mayo Clinic to no avail. A parishioner of his church gave him a copy of my book, *Change Your Voice, Change Your Life*, and he decided to seek my help. He stayed one month, undergoing intensive daily voice therapy. He recovered his speaking voice which he calls a miracle. He phones or writes periodically to report that his voice remains fully recovered. Here is his statement written May 19, 1989:

> As I consider Dr. Cooper's work, I see it as a ministry, providing help, hope and wholeness for people who have reached the point of giving up on ever communicating normally again. Dr. Cooper's therapy is simple but effective as he teaches us to use our voices the way God intended them to be. And as Dr. Cooper's techniques work wonders, there is a feeling of re-birth, not just for the voice but for the whole person. When you've come to believe that you have lost something forever . . . and then receive it back again, it is like a miracle. I can't describe the joy! And it has brought a new vitality to my ministry. It has been a source of inspiration for my people as they see hope for themselves in dealing with problems that once seemed hopeless. Through Dr. Cooper's therapy, he restores to those of us who had spastic dysphonia or other serious voice disorders the ability to experience again the very gift God has given us that makes us human: the gift of communication.

Zelda was in her twenty-eighth year as an elementary school teacher when she was told she would have to quit teaching permanently because of spastic dysphonia. She couldn't answer the telephone, let alone teach a class. She couldn't talk.

Zelda underwent two to three hours of intensive individual therapy every weekday, plus group therapy on Saturdays. As she improved, her sessions became less intense, but she continued on a daily basis. Today, Zelda is back teaching with a normal voice. Here is Zelda's comment:

> I knew Dr. Cooper could perform miracles when he cured my laryngitis (polyps) in three months—when I first came to him way back in 1970.
>
> When I couldn't find Dr. Cooper in April, 1985, during the onset of my spastic dysphonia, I went to my ENT doctor. When I asked him where Dr. Cooper was, he answered, "Oh, he's around." . . .
>
> The ENT doctor treated me with antibiotics and referred me to his voice pathologist, who gave me very little hope for recovery. In fact, he told me that many people with spastic dysphonia get discouraged and go in for surgery. That really scared me and made me determined to find Dr. Cooper.
>
> Fortunately for me, I did find Dr. Cooper and will be forever grateful to him for his expertise in treating my spastic dysphonia.

Rabbi Alan is being seen in my office at the present time. Here is his story:

> In January 1988, . . . I started to notice that my voice was "grabbing" on me. With the onset of any appreciable tension, my throat would close, my diaphragm would tighten, and my voice would become severely stifled. Over time, this phenomenon became progressively worse, particularly in public speaking situations, but carrying over into normal conversation as well. At this point, I began a desperate search for ways to restore my ability to speak and

communicate. I tried nutritional supplements; exercise; dieting; subliminal tapes; yoga; and meditation—all to no avail.

In February, 1989, I consulted a neurolaryngologist at the UCLA Medical Center. He diagnosed my problem as spastic dysphonia, a vocal disorder which many in the medical field consider a hopeless neurological condition. Needless to say, I came away from him depressed about my present prospects, and fearful about my future.

Then in April, 1989, I saw Dr. Morton Cooper for the first time. He informed me . . . that if I followed his simple recommendations, my prognosis was excellent. Working with me for less than three minutes, Dr. Cooper adjusted my voice placement and breathing so that I was able to enjoy several moments of normal, unstrained speech. I came away from Dr. Cooper feeling that my vocal problems were essentially simple, and that I could probably take care of the whole thing myself.

However, my condition continued to worsen. I began to cut off communication with my friends, family, and congregants, because speaking was so exhausting and embarrassing for me. I really sounded like a monster! Finally, in September, 1989, in a state of complete desperation, I decided to begin seeing Dr. Cooper on a regular basis. For the first six months of treatment, my progress was slow. Then in mid-March, 1990, I experienced a breakthrough. I realized that I could successfully perform what Dr. Cooper calls "self-monitoring." That is, when I sensed the onset of vocal tension, I made a conscious effort to employ Dr. Cooper's technique of placing my voice in "the mask" (the naso-pharyngeal cavity), and breathing. Once I accomplished this, I found that I could speak as normally and easily as anyone on the planet.

There is nothing magical or spectacular about Dr.

Cooper's approach to spastic dysphonia; nor is there anything terribly complicated about spastic dysphonia itself. While it sounds and even feels like some horrible affliction, I find, in reality, spastic dysphonia is nothing more than an elaborate form of stage fright, which manifests as involuntary squeezing of the lower throat and reversed breathing. Given the right combination of stress and tension, it is a behavior into which anyone could fall. But since spastic dysphonia is in fact ONLY a behavior, like any behavior, it is something that can be altered and eventually eliminated.

As someone who is 80% recovered from spastic dysphonia through the rigorous application of Dr. Cooper's techniques, I am living proof that this is true. I am now gaining a speaking voice which is actually more natural and powerful than it was before the onset of my condition. At this stage of progress, I feel tremendous gratitude to God, and to Dr. Cooper, whose unflagging kindness, patience, and support are enabling me to recover and enjoy my true, natural speaking voice.

No one should be put off by the apparent simplicity of Dr. Cooper's method. To paraphrase Albert Einstein: only when we simplify, are we truly able to speak with God.

The list of people who have found Direct Voice Rehabilitation helped them recover from spastic dysphonia is more extensive than space allows. Let me give you a few more personal accounts.

Spastic dysphonia is no respecter of age. Lisa was twenty-one when she was diagnosed as having spastic dysphonia. But let her tell her story:

A few years ago because of voice misuse, my vocal cords became very weak and when I would speak, I would lose ends of words and sentences. My voice was very much lower all of a sudden (to this day I blame it on the birth control pill). Anyway, I went to an Ear, Nose and Throat doctor in Beverly Hills. I was diagnosed with Spastic Dysphonia and told that if I didn't get better, I might have to have a throat operation.

The Doctor told me to "do things you like to do, play tennis, jog, whatever you like. I am going to prescribe Valium." . . . Soon afterwards, I started to pursue an acting career. When I was being critiqued after some scene work, I mentioned that I was having trouble with my voice. One of the students recommended that I go and see Dr. Morton Cooper.

When I went to Dr. Cooper, he told me that my voice was coming from the throat and that I was using shallow breathing. He simply taught me how to breathe from the diaphragm and to raise my voice up into the face mask area.

I later went to Europe to Drama School, where I again was taught this very same method—diaphragm breathing and resonance from the lips and face mask area.

Whenever I slip back to a low voice (usually out of laziness) doing the simple voice placement exercises—humming, etc., always works. These voice methods are no secret. They are taught world wide. I attended the Royal Academy of Dramatic Art in London.

Personally, I think that it is inappropriate to offer an operation as an alternative to this condition of spastic dysphonia. I met several people who had had this operation . . . and they were absolutely no better.

Finally, I think that Dr. Morton Cooper is practicing in a very simple, straightforward and effective way—which works, and can be backed up by any legitimate voice coach.

Don has a great sense of humor, even with spastic dysphonia; here is his account:

In January of 1989, having reached the point where at times I was unable to speak without sounding as though I were strangling on my own words, I went to see Dr. Morton Cooper.

Dr. Cooper expressed the opinion that I was suffering from a condition called spastic dysphonia but wanted me to see my own physician for an independent diagnosis.

I then went to see my Ear-Nose-Throat specialist, Dr. Edward Kantor. After extensive examinations, including fiber-optical pictures of my vocal cords, Dr. Kantor concluded that I was suffering from spastic dysphonia. He was of the opinion that my condition could be treated with vocal therapy and recommended that I return to Dr. Cooper for same.

Toward the end of January, I began biweekly therapy sessions with Dr. Cooper. I intensively practiced the principles he taught me, both in and away from his office, and within a month had reached the point where I was confident enough to ply my trade as an actor again.

The ideal ending to all this, of course, would be that after 25 years or so I became an overnight discovery and went on to star in my own TV series or movie. Being at the mercy of the vagaries of show business, however, this hasn't happened. Yet.

The important thing is that I am ready to work again because I have my voice back stronger than ever and, thanks to Dr. Cooper, I'm going to keep it.

There was nothing magical about my treatment, nor did it involve drugs or medicine, hypnosis, or any sort of invasive therapy. Dr. Cooper simply helped me find my own voice and showed me how to use it properly. This was accomplished through the use of certain vocal exercises and techniques taught by Dr. Cooper. It's that simple, and it's that great. . . .

And lest that sounds a bit formal and stodgy, I'd like to add my heartfelt thanks and gratitude and state for the record that I am a Dr. Cooper fan.

This account by Evert which he wrote in June 1989 is a very dramatic story:

My voice, both in music and in my profession, has been my life. Therefore, in 1981 when a slight tremor in my speaking voice began to occur, I became worried. It blossomed into a full-grown problem in Feb., 1982 while giving an Honorary Life Membership in the Parent Teacher Association to one of my deserving teachers. By the time I ended the presentation, it sounded as though I were going to cry. That was not true at all. Both my head and my voice shook but not from emotion. I just could not control them. I was examined by the doctor who had examined me for 25 years but he could find nothing wrong. He then referred me to a neurologist for a neurological workup. At first the neurologist thought I had Parkinson's Disease, but then he said, "No, you do not have Parkinson's because by intense concentration, you can control the shaking of your head. If you had Parkinson's, the head-shaking would be involuntary." He was able to tell me what I did not have but he was unable to diagnose my problem.

I was then referred to a speech therapist who compounded the problem by trying to get me to speak in a lower tone. She, too, finally said, "I can't help you."

In spite of my speech problem, after my retirement from The Los Angeles Unified School District, I became Assistant to the President of a college .... it is my responsibility to call on supporters of the college to thank them for their support and to give them an update on what is happening. The problem was that my voice was getting increasingly worse. In July, 1988 I was in the San Francisco area making calls for the college. I was having such a hard time controlling my voice and the shaking of my head that when I rang a doorbell, I prayed that no one would be home. That is a pretty sad state of affairs for a Public Relations position. I became very discouraged knowing that I would have to give up the retirement job which I had come to love because of the work the college is doing.

Through a series of fortuitous circumstances shortly after my trip to San Francisco, I was referred to Doctor Joseph Sugerman who diagnosed my condition as Spastic Dysphonia and then he said. "I believe you can be helped dramatically." Whereupon he referred me to Dr. Cooper for therapy.

My first session with Dr. Cooper was August 22, 1988. Since that time, the improvement in my voice has been dramatic and my head- shaking has stopped. I had what Dr. Cooper refers to as "a strangled voice," a condition which is caused by using the muscles in the lower throat to speak, rather than keeping the voice focused in "the mask" which includes the bridge and sides of the nose down to and around the lips.

An indication of the dramatic results which have occurred is the fact that I just recently completed a nine day tour of California with the president of the college in which we visited supporters of the college throughout the state of California. That never would have been possible without the help of Dr. Morton Cooper.

In closing, let me say that it is impossible for me to express adequately the gratitude I feel towards Dr. Cooper for restoring not only my voice, but my self-esteem as well. Without a doubt, I could not have continued my position with the college without his help. In fact, at the rate my ability to speak clearly and distinctly was decreasing, had I not met Dr. Cooper and received the benefit of his treatment, I probably would not be speaking at all at this time.

Shadoe Stevens, actor/producer, host of "American Top 40 Radio Show" wrote the following:

> It was like a miracle pain reliever. Dr. Cooper said: "Here's a quick and easy end to those voice nightmares." My voice was becoming strangled; I was losing control of my range and my tone. After years of discomfort, tension and stress, after studying with numerous voice coaches and suffering endless debilitating bimonthly throat infections, in a flash, almost overnight, Dr. Cooper's techniques changed my whole approach to using my voice. Almost by magic, my voice problems disappeared. It was astoundingly, hilariously simple and logical and it worked.

HOPELESS IS NOT HOPELESS AT ALL

To summarize, contrary to the prevailing opinion, spastic dysphonia, or what I call "the monster voice," isn't hopeless at all. It has an excellent prognosis in most cases, with Direct Voice Rehabilitation in my office. I differ with my colleagues and medical associates in treating spastic dysphonia, as well as other voice problems. But the successful results—and the recovered patients—speak for themselves.

The late Henry Fonda came to me complaining about his strangled voice. Through my program of Direct Voice Rehabilitation, he was able to recover his voice and go on to film *On Golden Pond*. He received an Academy Award for his role.

Henry Fonda, Dr. Don Dodson, Zelda, The Reverend Jim, and others whose conditions were diagnosed as irreversible have proven that "miracle cures" can happen. But they are not really miracle cures; they are the result of patient cooperation and the ability to follow directions based on simple, direct, natural techniques that any competent speech pathologist can utilize. Speech pathologists throughout the country and around the world can do what I am doing. I simplify. They can, too. The public benefits. The bottom line is, Direct Voice Rehabilitation has worked and can work.

VOCAL CORD PARALYSIS
(PARALYTIC DYSPHONIA)

Another serious voice problem is vocal cord paralysis. Recovering from surgery to remove a tumor from the thyroid gland, Rolf, M.D. found his voice was hoarse, lacked carrying power, and faded or failed within a few minutes of conversation. Rather than have a teflon injection into the paralyzed vocal cord, Dr. R. elected to try direct voice rehabilitation. His surgeon, William Longmire, M.D., UCLA Medical Center, referred him to me. I realized, from what Dr. R. told me, he had been having voice trouble before his surgery without knowing it. His voice had been failing and fading, but he assumed this was normal. I concluded it would take a year for him to regain his voice—a better voice than he had ever had. It took him one year, almost to the day. That was twenty years ago. Recently, Dr. R. was on my television show, speaking with the excellent voice he worked for and obtained many years ago. He said he never gets hoarse or loses his voice anymore. His voice is clear and efficient, yet he still has a paralyzed vocal cord. Not too long ago, I was a guest at his hospital. Some in the medical community found it hard to believe that Dr. R. had ever had a voice problem. But he and I both knew, since we had recordings of his old voice, that once upon a time he had had a very serious voice problem.

Let me tell you briefly about Steven, Ph.D. In January 1982, Dr. S. experienced a severe upper back pain and then tingling in his right hand. After some weeks of conservative therapy (placing him in traction), the decision was made that the "slipped disc" in the cervical (neck) area of his spine required surgery to relieve the pressure on the nerves which affected his hand/arm functioning. He awoke from surgery with a paralyzed tongue and vocal cord on the left side.

Dr. S. was immediately referred to an otolaryngologist for what was obviously laryngeal functioning damaged during the surgery, and to a neurologist to attempt to discern what nerves were affected and what might or could be done. An otolaryngologist was ready to do surgery: first a temporary gell-foam injection to give strength to the voice, with discussion about a more experimental nerve transplant operation mostly being done on animals.

During this period, now three months after his operation, Dr. S. had a barely audible voice. It was painful and tiring for him to speak, with a dryness and raspiness in his voice. Most of his professional activity had to be canceled. He did some teaching, using powerful amplification, but even with microphones, he had to cut back.

Another three months passed. Dr. S. traveled out-of-state for the second time to consult an expert, who gave quite a different reaction. While the expert expressed compassion and understanding of what Dr. S. was going through, he believed that the damage was permanent. Dr. S., he said, would have to face life with a paralyzed vocal cord, though a permanent teflon injection to the paralyzed cord might possibly help to increase the volume in his voice.

As the months wore on, Dr. S. vacillated between depression and coming to accept the possibly permanent condition on the one hand, and on the other hand, a greater desire to exert control over his own health and seek out alternatives, since the medical community seemed almost unable to help or give any consultative direction other than more surgery.

By now—ten months after his trauma-inducing surgery—Dr. S. was reading everything and anything he could find about voice therapy and voice rehabilitation. It so happened that at the university where he works, they were using my textbook, *Modern Techniques of Vocal Rehabilitation* (1973). Dr. S. got a copy and read it. He decided that it was imperative to come to Los Angeles and work with me.

Doctor after doctor had told Dr. S. that his condition was hopeless. In one year of voice rehabilitation with his flying in to see me periodically, he recovered his full normal voice. Says Dr. S.:

> Our society has not yet come to realize the pervasiveness of vocal impairment, much less the need to appreciate prevention and rehabilitation and therapy. Helen Keller helped the world understand much about impaired functions and human possibilities. Others have contributed to many advances related to hearing and vision impairment, rehabilitation, and prevention. I do not consider myself an evangelist on this topic. Yet I would be forever grateful if I could contribute minutely to the sensitivity, awareness and training possibilities of persons such as Dr. Morton Cooper. I have witnessed the joy given others as a result of successful vocal work. I know my own feelings of gratitude to Cooper and to the ability to regain a good voice.

In 1970, I published the results of my Direct Voice Rehabilitation with paralytic dysphonic patients in *California Medicine* and in *Eye, Ear, Nose and Throat Monthly*. Of the eighteen patients with a paralyzed vocal cord, fourteen were discharged with excellent results, fully recovered, and four with good results, being judged to be ninety percent recovered. Time spent in therapy for these eighteen patients was six to eighteen months. Since that time my success with this condition has continued to be good to excellent, and at times, therapy was completed in less than six months.

The so-called hopeless or impossible voice disorders are usually not that at all. The prognosis for having normal and effective voices again is usually excellent; if seen by a competent voice pathologist, these people should be able to successfully resume their careers and lives. No one should ever live with a voice problem when help is available. I have been called the "miracle voice doctor" by some of my patients. It has been my pleasure to be of assistance to them in recovering from what many have been told are hopeless voice problems. Spastic dysphonia, paralytic dysphonia, and growths on the vocal cords should not be treated by self-help. These are very serious voice disorders, and they require competent professional direction.

VOICE SUICIDE:
AN OCCUPATIONAL HAZARD

Joan Rivers asks, "Can we talk?"

I say "No!" America is committing voice suicide, but few know it.

What is voice suicide? It's the All-American game, our newest national pastime. I find fifty percent of voices around us are too thin, high pitched, or nasal, causing sound pollution. At least twenty-five percent are too low and guttural, causing voice suicide or voice burnout.

People everywhere are afflicted with it. You see and hear them every day; they are in the office, on the street, probably even in your own home. You could be one of them.

When you "push" your voice, perhaps to be heard over noise or to give directions to someone, does your voice drop so deep that your throat starts to hurt? Do you get laryngitis after a few hours of speaking in "authoritative" tones in person or on the phone? Does your throat tighten after speaking at office meetings or in front of large groups? Is your throat "tender" after yelling at the kids all day—or rooting for your favorite sports team? These problems, and others, come from committing voice burnout.

Too many Americans commit voice suicide by misusing or abusing their voices. They talk with weak ineffective voices that are too high and thin, too nasal, or too guttural and too deep in the throat. They have the symptoms of voice trouble, such as throat clearing, frequent laryngitis, hoarseness, or a voice that tires. Their necks ache after talking; speaking is an effort for them. Since the voice fades, they can talk only for limited periods, and then, not as well as they might like. They find it difficult to be listened to or heard.

Misusing your voice can lead to irritation of the vocal folds or cords, even leading to nodes, polyps, and contact ulcers. If the misuse is persistent or extensive, it may result in a premalignancy of the cords, such as papillomatosis or leukoplakia, and, finally, to cancer of the vocal cords. I find impaired voices such as the strangled (or monster) voice can, and often do, develop from use of the wrong voice.

Voice health is an essential issue with most entertainers. For people not in show business, it is another matter. These people know they need help but they don't know what to do or where to go, and they may be hesitant to spend money to correct the problem. There also is the prevailing myth that we are born with the voice we use, and that's it. The fact is most voices can be adjusted quickly and simply in a way that is completely natural and direct.

THEY'RE NOT LISTENING

Amy was told by four physicians and three speech pathologists that her voice was all but gone. When she asked the physicians what to do, she was advised to wait. Amy waited and her voice didn't come back. The speech pathologists had other suggestions, but nothing worked. Finally, she was repeatedly told, "Your voice isn't going to come back."

What I am saying is this: many medical professionals do not know how to listen to the voice. They presume that what ails the patient has to be seen, not heard.

An allergist may treat a patient who has a simple voice disorder, under the mistaken assumption, or presumption, that the voice is failing or has failed because of an allergy, when no such relationship prevails. An allergy may exist, but I find it minimally affects the speaking voice and its efficiency. (It may affect the quality but not really the basic efficiency.)

When a speaking voice fails, or is failing, many in the medical profession presume the problem is neurological or organic. If they can't find an organic or medical cause, one they can see, they fault the patient. The problem is considered to be psychosomatic, emotional or psychological. When the patient tries the psychiatric or emotional approach, and nothing is found, the patient is again faulted. The psychologist or psychiatrist also believes that the problem lies with the patient, not the diagnosis, which is presumed to be accurate. In most cases, the patient is not the failure. It is the diagnosis that sends the patient in the wrong direction.

Correct direction, along with voice psychotherapy (and psychotherapy as needed), is the key to recovery. Appropriate mechanical direction—a lower pitch, a higher pitch, a different tone, a change in resonance, better breath support—is *the* factor that enables the voice to recover, along with voice psychotherapy to help resolve the voice identity and voice image.

Unfortunately, I have often found the direction given a patient is not only inadequate, but lacking completion. In time, the patient is told his case or condition is hopeless or impossible—especially when categorized as spastic dysphonia, geriatric voice, bowed vocal cords, or a paralyzed vocal cord. It is often only the direction that is hopeless. For the patients, there is a prognosis of hope for ninety-nine percent of the cases I see.

Too often, the simple, corrective techniques are overlooked in favor of more complicated and bizarre methods, including so-called voodoo therapy. As mentioned earlier, one patient was told by his physician to chew on a golf ball for his spastic dysphonia (strangled voice). Another was told to change his liquor from scotch to bourbon, and when that didn't help, to have surgery.

All too often speech pathologists are not listening either. In my opinion, that is because they are not always well-trained in voice. Some simply do not know what direction to give patients with wrong or problem voices. There are documented cases of other experimental therapeutic techniques, such as working out in a darkened room, screeching like a donkey, endless hours of reading aloud from a book without direction, and muscle crunching workouts. Still another patient, Ric, was told to lift a chair high above his head as he had a paralyzed vocal cord. It didn't help. Direct Voice Rehabilitation worked, and the patient talked about his voice recovery on TV. In my experience, speech pathologists desperately want to learn how to do voice therapy. They need training and experience.

Over the years I found that it basically takes only seconds to determine an individual's real voice. Yet the majority of my colleagues said—and continue to say—that it takes months. To me this is a reversal of the procedure. To repeat again: Finding your natural voice often takes only seconds. Learning how to use and maintain the natural voice with correct mid-section breath support takes time and training until it can be automatic in various situations and with different people.

Voice improvement in a patient demands competency on the part of physicians and voice pathologists, as well as cooperation from patients. These two factors, competency and cooperation, offer an excellent prognosis to making voice recovery work.

SURGERY: THE GREAT AMERICAN PASTIME

The patient, a lady, had surgery for spastic dysphonia. The surgery was successful, only it didn't help her talk. She had a second operation and it too was a success, but she was still unable to talk. A nervous breakdown followed. She was recovering from that when her doctor advised her to have surgery again.

Another patient, also a woman, had been working with a speech pathologist for three years. The speech pathologist told her to read aloud from a book to correct her strangled voice. She was not told to raise or lower her pitch, how to focus her voice in the mask or how to breathe correctly, only to read aloud. When that didn't work, she had surgery. She was able to speak, but only in a breathy way because the surgeon had cut her laryngeal nerve, which paralyzed a vocal cord. Six months after that, she returned to her old spastic sound again.

Physicians should give options to the patient: surgery, or voice re-habilitation, or a combination. In addition, the negative as well as the positive aspects of surgery should be discussed.

Having surgery alone often just scratches the surface of the prob-lem, because the real cause—a troubled or failing voice—has basically been left untreated. If the voice problem returns, once more surgery may be recommended. The patient cannot be blamed for following the doctor's advice. We live in a "now" society. People want an im-mediate cure, and surgery is immediate. Essentially, surgery doesn't change a misused or abused voice. It may remove the tissue that formed on the vocal cords from using the wrong voice, but the pa-tient ultimately may need to learn a new correct voice.

I have been fortunate over the years to be associated with a small sophisticated group of ear, nose, and throat doctors who refer pa-tients for direct voice rehabilitation instead of surgery, or following surgery: Robert Adair, M.D., Donald Doyle, M.D., Robert Feder, M.D., Edward Kantor, M.D., Harvey Paley, M.D., Lawrence Pleet, M.D., Joel Pressman, M.D., Monte Purcelli, M.D., Alvin Reiter, M.D., Ronald Roth, M.D., Henry J. Rubin, M.D., Joel Shulman, M.D., Sher-man Strand, M.D., Joseph Sugerman, M.D., and Hans von Leden, M.D.

Other knowledgeable physicians that I have been privileged to work with in the treatment of voice and speech problems include: Benjamin Kagen, M.D., Gershon Lesser, M.D., William Longmire, M.D., Robert Rand, M.D., and David Rubin, M.D., among many oth-ers—too many to list but to whom I am grateful for the chance of working with them.

QUESTIONS & ANSWERS

Q: Can voice affect a person's physical and mental health?

A: Yes, voice has a definite effect on physical and mental health, for it influences not only careers but personal relationships. The properly used voice has a "feel good" sound. It builds confidence and makes a positive impression on others. A nat-ural, healthy voice can turn lives around.

Q: My three-year-old son is hard of hearing, and his speech is poor. Friends and associates have suggested that I wait until he is four or five for help with his speech, believing that he might outgrow the problem, at least, partially. I am fearful that I might be wasting valuable time, and hurting his chances for progress. What is your suggestion?

A: For a child with a hearing handicap, speech therapy, as well as auditory training, is not only appropriate but essential. There is a "speech readiness" period for a child. That is a time when the child develops his speech most fully, and most naturally. The hearing-handicapped child is deprived (to varying degrees) of natural and normal sound stimulation that hearing children have. Therefore, the hearing-handicapped child falls behind in speech ability and development. If you wait until he is four or five, you are allowing time to waste away and the speech readiness period to dissipate. Your son may outgrow some of his speech problem, but it is not likely, especially with a hearing problem. He needs sound stimulation and speech therapy now.

Q: Can a person who is severely hard of hearing have a normal voice?

A: A patient of mine from England told me that three almost deaf boys in her family all have normal voices. They were taught voice as well as speech from early childhood by the school system. In my office, by using the Voice Mirror Machine and the hum technique, individuals who are severely hard of hearing can be helped to have normal voices.

Q: I recently read about an experimental vocal cord injection technique to help patients with spastic dysphonia. Does it work?

A: You are referring to an experimental procedure used in some hospitals, whereby the patient's vocal cord is injected with botulinum, an invasive toxic substance. Botulinum is a diluted form of the deadly botulism. The downside and side effects affecting the body, as well as the vocal cord, are not fully known. The procedure causes a temporary parasis or pa-

ralysis rather than a permanent paralysis of the vocal cord
and generally appears to involve repeated doses. It was origi-
nally thought that the injection would last nine months, but
the period may be reduced to six months, three months, or
six weeks.

Q: My voice is often tired. No one believes me. They say it is in
my mind. I keep telling them it is in my throat. Who is right?

A: You are. Misuse of the voice by incorrect pitch, improper
tone focus and poor breath support results in a "tired voice."
The throat aches, and many allied symptoms may result. The
reason no one believes you when you say your voice tires is
because most people are unaware of the speaking voice, and
the symptoms of voice misuse. From time to time your voice
may become tired from fatigue or lack of sleep, but if you use
your voice well it should remain clear and easy.

Q: My doctor tells me I have a growth on my vocal cord called
"papilloma." He advises surgery, but I don't want surgery.
What do you advise?

A: Vocal misuse and abuse, I have found, may contribute to the
onset and development of the kind of growth you have. In
1971 at UCLA Medical Center, my study revealed that within
a period of three months, four out of eight patients with
biopsied papillomata of the vocal cords either reduced or
eliminated the growths through Direct Voice Rehabilitation—
change of pitch, tone focus, breathing, and voice hygiene;
these findings were published in the *Journal of Speech and
Hearing Disorders*.

Q: How can you tell when a voice is going wrong?

A: By the symptoms. You get hoarse, your voice doesn't hold up
throughout the day, your voice fades (people continually ask
you to repeat yourself), your throat aches, or you find you
have to push your voice. If you have any of these symptoms,
you may be committing voice suicide without even knowing
it.

Q: I was told I had two growths called "polyps" on my vocal cords. My doctor suggested an inhaler. I tried one and it didn't work. I then tried pills, shots, gargles, voice rest, and even bed rest. Now, because all these things failed, I have been advised to change my job. I am a salesman and I love my work. What do you recommend?

A: Polyps are benign growths on the vocal cords. Surgery can remove polyps, but since voice misuse—the wrong pitch, quality, volume, and placement of the voice—often creates them, it is essential you learn how to use your speaking voice. These growths have responded extremely well to voice therapy. But if you choose not to learn correct voice usage, you will most likely continue to experience voice difficulty. My advice is: Do not change your job. Change the way you are using your voice.

Q: I have been advised to seek voice therapy following the surgical removal of two small nodules on my vocal cords. Why doesn't the surgery take care of the problem?

A: Surgery removes only the immediate problem. The real problem that caused the nodules was voice misuse and abuse. If you don't want a possible return of the nodules, you need to learn to use your voice properly. Without voice rehabilitation you might find yourself in need of the same surgical procedure again. Direct Voice Rehabilitation requires a voice pathologist who is knowledgeable and sophisticated to determine correct voice rehabilitation for the patient.

Chapter 10

Winning Voice Tips

THE VOICE OF SUCCESS

Not long ago, a young man looked me in the eyes and said, "I want the voice of success."

He was a salesman, and a good one, but he wanted to be even better. He wanted to be the best. It wasn't that his voice was poor. All it needed was fine tuning to give him a competitive edge.

"If my voice doesn't give the impression that I know what I'm talking about, my clients write me off immediately," he said. "I am on the phone constantly, so it is important that people *hear* what I have to say. My voice is my future. Without a voice that projects confidence and success, I'll never be the person I want to be. And *can* be."

The young man wasn't being boastful or dramatic. He simply knew what he wanted for his life. And there are millions more just like him. Everyone wants to be a winner. Not just now and then, but all the time. It's the American Dream.

Your voice has the power to make you a winner. It can make sure you are heard, listened to, and liked. It can gain you respect, get you a job, a husband or a wife. The right voice can make you admired and help you win friends. A wrong voice, on the other hand, can cause you to be misunderstood, rejected, even fired. It can close doors. The most correct and elegant language loses all its beauty with a bad or ill-trained voice.

159

No matter what level of success you have reached, professionally or personally, you can achieve more with a voice that commands respect and attention.

If you haven't been a winner, ask yourself *why not?*

Is your voice holding you back? Does it trouble you when you hear yourself? Do you feel insecure when you speak? Does your voice fade and give out? Does it prevent you from being who you are, or who you want to be?

If you feel good about your voice—and, equally important, it feels good when you use it—don't bother trying to make it better. But if you feel uncomfortable, you are speaking with the wrong voice.

SUMMING UP THE SECRETS OF VOICE

Talk in the mask, the area about your lips and nose, where all voices should come from. The mask brings out the subliminal hypnotic sound that makes the voice so likable and easy to listen to. All great voices have that sound placement and tone.

Use the buzz words to bring your voice forward. Practice your new voice as you read a book or newspaper. Say "um-hmm" as you respond in conversation. If your voice is too soft, increase your volume without forcing it. And be sure to monitor your daily progress on a tape recorder.

Breathe right, speak right. Breathe easy, from the stomach not the chest, please. Belly breathing is the way to go. Talking on air is like riding on tires with air, comfortable and comforting. As you talk, feel your stomach move in progressively, gradually, and smoothly.

How is your phone voice? Most of us have different voices for different occasions. We are voice schizophrenics, but never fear. It is normal and natural. The phone gets us to change our voices. We talk too loud or too soft, and often too low. Talk naturally. Be yourself. Don't talk in the lower throat, and don't go too loud.

If people think you aren't loud enough, or they frequently ask you to repeat yourself, speak up by pretending the other person is a little hard of hearing. People with soft voices have the ability to project. But too often, they let their voices sink down in the lower throat rather than project from the mask.

Shape up your voice quickly. You can get a voice tune up in seconds. Humming is a simple and direct way to help you find and use your natural voice—the voice that gets you heard, listened to , and liked.

Press your magic button (the Cooper Instant Voice Press). Raise your hands above your head and say the buzz words. Hum the first line of "Happy Birthday" or "Row, Row, Row Your Boat." Those exercises could not be more basic, yet they should help you find your natural voice, and relocate it whenever you are in doubt. Practice for seconds at a time throughout the day, until your new voice becomes second nature to you.

Try your natural, true voice on for size. Henry Fonda did it. Anne Bancroft, Dennis Weaver, Joan Rivers, and Cheryl Ladd did it. So did Cathy, Larry, Tom and Tobi. These people, and many others, have discovered their natural voices, and how to apply them to enhance their careers, and ultimately, their lives.

Within each of us exists a "star-quality" voice. Follow the simple plan described on these pages and you should find yours. Once you do, you can be on your way to Winning With Your Voice. Remember, I can help you find your natural voice, but you are the person that makes the rest happen. It is basically all up to you.

Bibliography

Books

Cooper, Morton. *Winning With Your Voice*. Hollywood, FL: Frederick Fell Publishers, Inc., 1989.

_____. *Change Your Voice, Change Your Life*. New York: Macmillan Publishing Company,1984. Paperback—New York: Harper & Row, Publishers, 1985.

_____. *Modern Techniques of Vocal Rehabilitation*. Springfield, IL: Charles C Thomas, 1973.

_____. and Marcia Cooper, (eds.). *Approaches to Vocal Rehabilitation*. Springfield, IL: Charles C Thomas, 1977.

Chapters

Cooper, Morton. "Treatment of Functional Aphonia and Dysphonia," in Perkins, William (ed.) *Current Therapy of Communication Disorders*. New York: Thieme & Stratton, Inc., 1983.

_____. "Modern Techniques of Vocal Rehabilitation for Functional and Organic Dysphonias," in Travis, L.E. (ed.). *Handbook of Speech Pathology and Audiology*. New York: Appleton-Century-Crofts, 1971.

_____. "Management of Voice, Speech, and Language Disorders," in Gellis, S.S. and Kagan, B.M. (eds.). *Current Pediatric Therapy*. 9th ed. Philadelphia: W.B. Saunders Company, 1980. (Also 8th ed., 1978; 7th ed., 1976; 6th ed., 1973)

Proceedings

Cooper, Morton. "Recovery from Spastic Dysphonia by Direct Voice Rehabilitation," *Proceedings of the 18th Congress of the International Association of Logopedics and Phoniatrics*, 1 (August 1980), 579-584.

Audio Digest
Cooper, Morton. "Techniques of Vocal Rehabilitation for Functional and Organic Voice Disorders," in Bradford, Larry and Robert Wertz (eds.). *Communicative Disorder: An Audio Journal for Continuing Education*, 4 (March 1979), Grune and Stratton, Inc.

Articles
Cooper, Morton. "Change Your Voice, Change Your Life," *Cosmopolitan* (July 1984), 138–142.

_____. "Prescriptions for Vocal Health: Finding the Right Vocal Register," *Music Educators Journal*, 69 (Feb.1983), 40, 57, 59, 61.

_____."Prescriptions for Vocal Health: Medication and the Voice," *Music Educators Journal*, 69 (Feb. 1983), 41–42.

_____. "The Tired Speaking Voice and the Negative Effect on the Singing Voice," *The Nats Bulletin*, 39 (Nov./Dec. 1982), 11–13.

_____. "A Case History: Stevie Nicks," *Voice*, 4 (Sept./Oct.1980), 34.

_____. "Vocal Image and Vocal Identity," *Voice*, 3 (July/Aug.1980) 36.

_____. "Facts and Fantasies About the Speaking Voice and the Effect Upon the Singing Voice," *Voice*, 2 (May/June 1980), 34.

_____. "The Speaking Voice of the Singer," *Voice*, 1 (Mar./Apr.1980), 8–11.

_____. "The Strangled Voice," *Let's Live*, 48 (Jan.1980), 71–76.

_____. "Aphasia - When the Words Don't Come Out Right," *Let's Live*, 47 (Sept.1979), 90,93, 94, 96.

_____. "The Impressive Voice in the Court," *Trial*, 15 (July 1979), 53–55, 69.

_____. "The Voice Problems of Stutterers: A Practical Approach from Clinical Experience," *Journal of Fluency Disorders*, 4 (June 1979), 141–148.

_____. "Be Good to Your Voice," *Prevention*, 31 (May 1979), 142–147.

_____. "The Secret Stutterers," *Let's Live*, 47 (May 1979).

_____. "The Speaking Voice and the Trial Lawyer," *Advocate*, 6 (Dec.1978), 11–13.

_____. "Spectographic Analysis of Fundamental Frequency and Hoarseness Before and After Vocal Rehabilitation," *Journal of Speech and Hearing Disorders*, 39 (Aug.1974), 286–297.

_____. "Preventing Voice Disorders," *United Teacher*, 4 (Sept.1972), 13.

_____. "The Stage Voice," *Equity*, LVII (Mar.1972), 21–22.

_____. "Speech Disorders and Problems," (Aphasia), *Pediatric News*, 6 (Jan.1972), 21.

_____. "Speech Disorders and Problems," (Stuttering), *Pediatric News*, 5 (Nov.1971) 55–56.

_____. "The Vocal Image and Vocal Suicide," *Voices: The Art and Science of Psychotherapy*, Special Issue: Unspoken Behavior, 6 (Aug.1971), 26–28.

_____. "Speech Disorders and Problems" (Voice Disorders), *Pediatric News*, 5 (Mar.1971) 48–49.

_____. "Papillomata of the Vocal Folds: I. Review of the Literature, II. A Program of Vocal Rehabilitation," *Journal of Speech and Hearing Disorders*, 36 (Feb.1971), 51–60

_____. "Rehabilitation of Paralytic Dysphonia," *Eye, Ear, Nose and Throat Monthly*, 49 (Dec.1970), 532–535.

_____. "Vocal Suicide in Newscasters and Announcers - The 'Impressive' Voice," *Radio-Television News Directors Association Bulletin* (Dec.1970), 21.

_____. "Stopping Vocal Suicide Among Preachers," *Christian Advocate* (Dec.1970), 11–12.

_____. "Voice Therapy for Teachers," *Education*, 91 (Nov./Dec.1970), 142–146.

_____. "A Broadcaster's Artistic Voice," *The Quill*, 58 (Oct.1970), 19.

_____. "Vocal Suicide Among Rabbis," *Central Conference of American Rabbis Journal*, 17 (Oct.1970),70–73.

_____. "Vocal Suicide of the Speaking Voice in Singers," *Music Educators Journal*, 57 (Sept.1970), 53–54.

_____. "Vocal Suicide Among Theologians," *Your Church*, 3 (July/Aug.1970), 16–21.

_____. "Voice Problems of the Geriatric Patient," *Geriatrics*, 25 (June 1970), 107–110.

_____. "Voice Suicide in Teachers," *Peabody Journal of Education*, 47 (May 1970), 334–337.

_____. "Speech Disorders and Problems" (Part I), *Pediatric News*, 4 (Mar.1970), 16, 37.

_____. "Speech Disorders and Problems" (Part II), *Pediatric News*, 4 (Apr.1970), 27, 57.

_____. "Speech Disorders and Problems" (Part III), *Pediatric News*, 4 (May 1970), 27, 48.

_____. "Teacher, Save That Voice!" *Grade Teacher*, 87 (Mar.1970), 71–72, 74, 76.

_____. "Vocal Suicide in Singers," *The Nats Bulletin*, 26 (Feb./Mar.1970), 7–10, 31.

_____. "Vocal Rehabilitation - Current Opinion," *Medical Tribune*, 11 (Feb. 23, 1970), 11.

_____. "Vocal Suicide in the Legal Profession," *Bar Bulletin*, 43 (1968), 453–456. Reprinted in *Case and Comment*, 75 (Jan./Feb. 1970), 44–47.

_____. "Rehabilitation of Paralytic Dysphonia," .*California Medicine*, 112 (Jan.1970), 18–20.

_____. "Vocal Suicide in the Theatrical Profession," *The Screen Actor*, 11 (Nov./Dec.1969), 8–9.

_____. "In Consultation," *Medical Tribune*, 10 (Aug. 28, 1969), 13.

_____. and Naoaki Yanagihara, "A Study of Basal Pitch Level Variations Found in the Normal Speaking Voice of Males and Females," *Journal of Communication Disorders, 3 (1971), 261*–266.

_____. and Alan M. Nahum. "Vocal Rehabilitation for Contact Ulcer of the Larynx," *Archives of Otolaryngology*, 85 (1967), 41–46.

Satou, Alan and Morton Cooper. "Psychiatric Observations of Falsetto Voice," *The Voice*, 17 (Feb.1968), 31–33, 35, 37, 39, 41.

Column

Voice Disorders: Questions and Answers with Dr. Cooper, *United Teacher*, 1973–1975.